Works Volume 1

by Nicholas Jay Boyes

www.ecologicalera.com

contactnicholas@ecologicalera.com

ISBN: 978-0-557-13363-5

Table of Contents

Introduction

This works edition is a collection of articles written by me in the course of about 2 years. It is a reflection of the conditions of the American Democratic Republic. At the time of writing this introduction, the United States stock market crashed. Stocks experienced their greatest loss in one week in history, and the recession was definitely occurring.

A variety of economic conditions led to the fall, from the speculation on variable rate mortgages, the start of the crisis, to the inability of America to industrialize properly, in particular the failure of the country to convert to the metric system.

The latter was of note as the age of disposable products was reaching a conclusion in the new millennium, and non metric parts had but one source, America. Thus the rejection of the disposable products due to the detrimental effects on the ecology seriously damaged American industry.

It marks the fall of an empire, and it is stil not clear whether it will be able to get up again. One thing is clear: if and when it does it will be looking quite a bit different than it previously did, poorer, and less commanding.

Thus we begin Works volume 1.

Chapter 1

Chicago Recycling by Nicholas Jay Boyes 10 21 2006

Chicago has moved one step closer towards a 100% recycling programme for the downtown regions. Wards two and five will be given blue cans to recycle their wastes, both downtown Chicago. The new way of recycling will replace the last system of blue bags placed in the garbage which was simply not as effective as the blue cans.

The proletariat of Chicago will not be left behind and kept in a backwards industrial condition for the sake of surplus value. Chicago only recycles 8% of its garbage currently, a real shame for the workers and ecology. The bourgeois of Chicago has said in the past they wanted 25% of the garbage recycled, but clearly a push was needed.

The proletariat of Milwaukee, who have achieved 100% recycling of Aluminum, Steel, HDPE 1 and PETE 2, Glass, Corrugated Cardboard, and Paper in all of its regions, with the blue can method, has lessons for Chicago. Milwaukee may be small compared to Chicago, but it has industry and a proletariat. Recycling has proved to be a responsible method of eliminating unwanted waste for Milwaukee.

The benefit of the blue cans for Chicago is the recyclables no longer go with the urban trash, and will have a separate pickup. For the worker who has to sort and bale the recyclables, this represents a major advancement. It is a dirty hard job to bale the cans, but it is a rewarding one. The baler uses a hydraulic system to make the cans into bales, and they are then loaded onto the truck trailers or boxcars. After this the cans go to be smelted, in Indiana where they are made into ingots, and sold as raw steel or Aluminum for industry.

The recycling of materials results in a higher quality less costly finished product. Its like finding a vein of Aluminum that is 100% pure. Obviously this method of industry costs less in production, and the ecological benefits are tremendous.

In Wisconsin the difference to the ecosystem is clearly evident in the forests of the north. In these temperate forests the need to log has decreased from paper recycling. The result of this is more rain for Chicago and Milwaukee. It may be a coincidence but this year (2006) Chicago had more rain than it had for a hundred years. It is obvious trees are one of the main drivers of the rains that come in the Great Lakes region. The fact they are being logged less is absolutely a factor in the increase of rainfall in the Chicago region.

Milwaukee's proletariat welcomes Chicago's workers efforts to recycle downtown. It is of international importance to have a recycling programme, and hopefully all help will be given by Milwaukee's bourgeoisie, who have control of the capital, to help Chicago to recycle. The proletariat must not stop here though, a 100% recycling programme is still required. Nevertheless this represents progress, and it is welcome.

See Chicago Tribune, 10 21 2006,
Article By Dan Mihalopoulos and Laurie Cohen
Tribune staff reporters

http://www.chicagotribune.com/news/local/chi-0
610210206oct21,1,806843.story?coll=chi-newsloca
l-hed&ctrack=1&cset=true

Nicholas Jay Boyes
Milwaukee Wisconsin USA
October 21 2006

On Ecological Restoration by Nicholas Jay Boyes 10 14 2006

The need to alter the relationship of man to nature is currently felt at its
most acute level in the equatorial regions of the world. In these regions,
from Mexico to the middle east and even China are becoming deserts
quickly. Serious efforts to restore the ecosystem are desperately needed
in the areas destroyed by mankind's anthropocentric search for wealth,
the likes of which were in the traditional method of man versus nature.

In the deserted areas the plants of the new world are going to be the
means by which the ecosystem is going to be fixed. By using the vast
resources of the new world, which range from the arid regions of Texas
and South Dakota to the rainforests of Washington, and the temperate
forests of Wisconsin, the ability of the proletariat to transform the desert
to green plains and even forest in many areas must be a solid goal of all
people.

Achieving the ecological transformation is going to require heavy
industry. Detroit could become a center for the production of the Earth
moving equipment that are a necessity to the building of terraces and
drilling of wells on the unstable eroding lands of hills and mountains,
and the plains of the Sahara where soil will have to be mined for. Heavy
machinery to mine soil from the north and move it to the south will be
one of the mainstays of the economy in these deserted areas.

Simply attempting to grow crops with fertilizers and pesticides will not
work in these desert regions. The overriding object must be to create
ecosystems that will simply grow without constant efforts and labor. In
this respect the efforts of the proletariat loom large, as only they can
correct the constant quest for production of surplus value, which drove
forward much of the ecological destruction we experienced in the
previous millennium. The Soviet socialists were also guilty of ecological
destruction, all the more reason for the proletariat to consider the efforts
of the ecological men of value, even if at first it seem non economic.

The ecological restoration of the equatorial areas is also going to require
labor. Some of it can come from the desert regions, but much of the
knowledge of how to drill the wells and move the soil will have to come

from the wealthy countries of the north. It could be considered an alternative to military service, whereby the non violent proletariat in countries that conscript are given the right not to kill other people in war, and, rather, work on the soil.

The benefits that come from less logging and more recycling, two things which must have been occurring in the new world, are more rains. This year, 2006, Chicago had more rain than it had since records were kept in the 1900s. The only thing different Wisconsin has done to cause this, as they are upwind from Chicago, is log less in the temperate forest. The change to computers from newspapers is one of the main shifts in the ecology of Wisconsin. Also, the recycling industry with newspapers and corrugated cardboard pickup from all people has removed the need to log greatly. With more rain crops are larger, and although it is hard to gauge as of yet the true benefits to society, if we were to rely on this year as a standard and start, Chicago would be in a position to greatly increase its economic strength, simply through more intense farming methods.

The coming push to correct the failures of the anthropocentric ways of man is occurring in the industrialized countries. Anarchy, with men being tribal, will never tap the true potential of man in the factory, the current social being of modern society. Thus we are left to the proletariat, who will provide the labor to fix the destruction of the areas previously inhabited. It is a task that can be accomplished, by changing our view of productive labor, and through the efforts of the individual proletariat to do things like garden coniferous trees for his area. The benefits of doing this will be more rain, and this could help the farm. And it should give us all peace of mind we are no longer a burden of the ecosystem, but an asset.

Nicholas Jay Boyes
Milwaukee Wisconsin USA
October 14 2006

On the Metric System in America by Nicholas Jay Boyes 10 4 2006

The United States remains the last industrialized country in the world, and one of the last even including with the third world, to officially make a metric conversion. In America the conversion from English to metric simply has not occurred in most heavy industry, and is not even mentioned by the official bourgeois leadership.

The British, whom were the founders of the current system of measurement, were among the last European nations too shift to the metric system in the late 20th century. Canada also shifted to the metric system around this time. All European countries had completed the shift to metric by the end of the 20th century.

The main reason for the inability of the bourgeoisie of America to change to metric is its main proponents are socialists. The socialists have been fighting with the bourgeoisie for so long now to do a metric conversion, it seems like eternity. The socialists have been through a variety of modern warfare techniques in the Milwaukee area from the government of the United States for their support of the metric system. It would be a surprise to see the eternal relations of capital change for a small group of political economists.

Given the fact the Universities hate the socialists too any meaningful discussion of the topic there is futile. Students are violently kicked out of Universities such as the University of Wisconsin for their support of the metric system. They continue to oppose any efforts by the proletarian youth to change to metric. Thus the shift to metric must occur in the factory, and later the University in America. It is a telling example of the backwardness of the so called betters of the working classes, whose institutions keep producing the same dull diplomats and psychiatric wardens to rule over the proletariat.

The proletarian people are the key to making the metric conversion in the factory. In the labor union the metric system should be discussed. Preparations for the coming shift to metric technology must be made at the ground level on the factory floor, with workers comprehending the units prior to and during the conversion. They are the best hope for a new future that has the more scientific system of measurement.

The upper classes in America will never out of the goodness of their hearts move to convert their factories to metric. It is a task that falls to the workers of the United States. It is a goal that can and will be achieved, and it will be the socialists who lead the movement, in the factory.

Nicholas Jay Boyes
Milwaukee Wisconsin USA
October 4 2006

On World War Two by Nicholas Jay Boyes 9 29 2006

There is much talk today about the class struggle that occurred in Europe in the last century. Many people seem to think they can support a few key battles and still have the respect of their countrymen, many of whom had relatives who either fought or rebuilt Europe after the Second World War. The truth of the matter is this: You either are for all of the war, or you are for none of it. Just because you support one or two of the main leaders, i.e. Franklin Delano Roosevelt, does not truly put you in the real revolution. You either support the Allied forces in World War Two, Franklin Delano Roosevelt, Winston Churchill, Joseph Stalin, and Harry Truman or you do not.

One would not say today he supported Benito Mussolini but not Adolf Hitler and expect support, even from the forces of the Axis. Clearly supporting the Nazis means support of Japan under Emperor Hirohito, Benito Mussolini of Italy, and Adolf Hitler of Germany.

If you support the Allied powers in World War Two, you are in favor of Franklin Delano Roosevelt of the United States of America, Winston Churchill of Great Britain, and Joseph Stalin of the Soviet Union.

All attempts to divide the unity of the Allies will fail if the proletariat stays together. Those who enjoy the gains of the battle and feel they cannot support the whole thing should either stay out of it, and not call themselves Allied, rather, neutral, or just face up to the fact by not respecting all the leadership of the Allies you are most likely, whether or not you are aware of it, Nazis.

The unfortunate truth about America today is most people are totally ignorant of the glorious class struggle that occurred in the 20th century. The holocaust is remembered by few, and those who do fail to see the entire picture, in particular the eastern front. Many of the same old clichés of the power of the German SS remains strong in the United States. A reactionary bourgeoisie that continues to disrespect the memories of the older generation, many of who they have forced to oppress workers by holding stock for retirement, displays a tragic state of affairs for the older generations of today's America.

To go abroad not knowing the true nature of the conditions of the struggles of a people, and to claim to desire to become part of it, is a statement of ignorance. Too many diplomats understand little of nothing about the people they claim to represent, and only serve as an embarrassment to the proletariat. These people assess the crises in America as momentary failures, rather than structural failure of the economic system. They never really see the true nature of the relationships present in capitalist society, and only pay lip service to the proletariat.

The proletariat is not so easily fooled. Realization of the fact many people in the country no longer support the Allies is coming. We can never go back to this violent time in American and European society, or call up the old slogans and hope to conquer the curses of wage labor. What we can do is learn and reassess our current conditions, and try to move forward with the knowledge the world once had unity, and as long as we remember, it remains.

Nicholas Jay Boyes
Milwaukee Wisconsin USA
September 29 2006

On Development of the Productive Forces in the Recycling Industry by Nicholas Jay Boyes 9 24 2006

The development of the productive forces in the recycling industry, brought about through the cooperative efforts of the masses, whose successful pickup and recycling movement has caused the creation of a new kind of commodity, post consumer materials, is the cause of a new form of socialism. This powerful environmental movement has enabled the workers to be the sole providers of raw materials to many industries, especially aluminum production.

As the only production cost is the pickup and baling of the materials prior to smelting, the resources are practically free. This has been possible due to the historical context, by the ability of machinery to use this new raw material in the factory. The aluminum baler, for example, is responsible for the expansion of the recycling industry on a massive scale. Using hydraulics previously unavailable to the industry, in a small machine literally thousands of tonnes of aluminum can be baled over time.

The role of the proletariat in recycling could not be greater. He not only uses his labor to sort the recyclables from home that are destined to be used as raw materials for the industry, he also works in the factories as wage labor to produce commodities with the recovered materials he produced.

The socialist aspect of this is the fact, through organizing the masses, the recycling movement is largely a costless industry. The only cost is the pickup and baling of the recovered resources. The recyclable materials, once sorted from household garbage, are free for the taking for the industry, i.e. steel. This movement to cause resources to be free is entirely within keeping with the socialist viewpoint. It may not create the outward signs of socialism, i.e. free health care, it is a heavy industrial socialism, where the raw materials for factories are so cheap it is practically free. Many industries, for example tire recycling, use materials that were a burden to the environment translating into storage costs for capitalists. With the new machinery, they ask no price. Furthermore it would be ridiculous to pay the producers of the materials, the masses, a few cents for their recyclables. That would be a return to the old days when people used their own means to recycle their goods, i.e. aluminum cans. For obvious reasons this is unlikely, cementing the successes of the recycling movement. development of the productive forces in industry, this production cost becomes an economic asset to be shared with society.

The heavy industrial socialism brought about through the more efficient use of materials, centered in the recycling industry, has totally transformed many regions in America. Even if the industry moves to 100% surplus value production in pick up and baling, the fact remains the raw material has been created by the environmental socialist proletariat.

Nicholas Jay Boyes
Milwaukee Wisconsin USA
September 24 2006

On the Nazis and the 20th Century by Nicholas Jay Boyes 9 7 2006

In the last century a class struggle raged between the forces of the old world and the new world, among revolutionaries and those who clung to their traditional old ways of life. This conflict of notions about the path for which society was to take was to culminate in a climax in the Second World War. In this period of the 20th century the forces of the bourgeoisie, the Nazi Fascist movement primarily from Germany under the reactionary Adolf Hitler, fought a pitched battle over the path which the future would take. On one side was the proletariat, the other side the bourgeoisie. The brutal struggle of body on body recognized by Karl Marx in the 19th century as the ultimate end of the capitalist period was reached in Germany in the 1940's. It was a product of the class struggle for many years in Western Europe, and its end was a victorious working class movement under the socialists.

The role of the British and the New World, was of international importance. The lack of ignorance of the nature of the old world Christian cultures of Western Europe played a decisive role, with the Americans and the British, although still bourgeois, playing the part of international forces revulsed by the degree of Nazi atrocities to the proletariat, many of whom had fled to the New World in the past through Britain. Their role, especially the British one, was of paramount importance to the growth of the socialist movement in the east and the west. The British were the civilized world where the class struggle was less developed in many ways, therefore not as thoroughly ingrained into the mind of the British as the Germans, and most likely not as important to the British as the Germans.

The Germans under Hitler staked their whole fate on the triumph of capitalism, limited universal suffrage, and Christianity over the equality of communism. Democracy as envisioned by Hitler, monolithic in its pull to the capitalist powers, was used very effectively as a propaganda apparatus to the appointed by the court, yet later elected by the people in a climate of fear, leader of the German people. The failure of Hitler to convince the proletariat of his connection to universal suffrage was one of the main forces behind the involvement of the British and Americans in the revolution that eventually toppled his government. By moving towards greater equality through universal suffrage, and through the socialist revolution of the Soviets, briefly the world had unity in its battle against the forces of the old world bourgeoisie. It was a fleeting moment though, as when the class dimensions of the struggle engaged in by the British and the Americans became less about the human rights of the workers, and more about what would follow the insurrection in Germany, the Americans and the British lost their nerve, resulting in the later arms race between the socialist and capitalist powers.

The presence of characters like General Christian, a leader of the Nazi Army in the last days of Hitler, Joseph Goebells, the Jesuit, Martin Bormann, the bourgeois bureaucrat, point to a history of an Old World slowly perishing under the weight of the workers, from their migration to the New World, and their revolutionary transformation in Russia and the Soviet Union. Ignorance of the Germans towards the fate of the exiles was of crucial importance to the struggle waged in the war, when many of the Germans forced to migrate, i.e. Albert Einstein, became very influential in proletarian circles. The failure of the Germans to allow for the real emancipation of the people from the Old World capitalist ideas was the cause of the failure of the government of Adolf Hitler. In its last days the communists would be put down violently with powder and lead, the true aims of Hitler's bourgeoisie from the start, the total conquering of the working class socialist movement, in the form of the Third International in the Soviet Union, and the new home of the exiled and shunned working class of Germans, the Americans, and the conduit, the British.

The real history of the Nazis and the last days of Hitler remains a topic of heated discussion, as those opposed to socialist ideas attempt to divide the people from the unity enjoyed in those fateful days of the war, when the New World, the British, and the Third International were one. It was no mistake that the leadership of America in those days was more tolerant of communism. It was a true feeling from the millions who came to America fleeing the monopolies of capital driving them to their economic and political migration. In a country that professes to have enjoyed universal suffrage, peace with the socialists of this time should be expected. The attempts of the current capitalist leadership to divide the people and suggest Joseph Stalin, Franklin Delano Roosevelt, Harry

Truman, and Winston Churchill were not united in those times, is but historic revisionism. It is folly to suggest those chaps were anything but together, given the scale of sacrifice put forward by the forces of the Allied movement. For all people, pacifist or not, we must learn from the past and read the works of H. Trevor Roper, Joseph Stalin, and many others who were involved in this chapter of history. It is of paramount importance to familiarize ones self with the true history of the 20th century, especially the war. It is a duty, and the proletariat must take it up, not as tradition, but as the building blocks of future revolutionary thought.

See H. Trevor Roper: The Last Days of Adolf Hitler for the British opinion of the revolution in Germany of the 20th century.

Nicholas Jay Boyes
Milwaukee Wisconsin USA
September 7 2006

Chapter 2

On the Condition of Children in the American Democratic Republic by Nicholas Jay Boyes 3 21 2007

The Organization for Economic Cooperation and Development (OECD) places together 30 member countries sharing a commitment to democratic government and capital. With active relationships with some 70 other countries and economies, NGO's (non government organizations) and civil society, it has a global reach. It is well known for its publications and its statistics, its work covers economic and social issues from macroeconomics, to trade, education, development and science and innovation. It is active with the United Nations UNICEF, and recently, in 2007, a report was made available on the web about the conditions of children in all the 30 countries, mostly European but also with America and Canada included. It can be accessed at the UNICEF website:

UNICEF's report can be accessed via this PDF file:

http://www.unicef.org/media/files/ChildPovertyReport.pdf

Here is how the United States fared compared to the rest of the industrialized world:

According to the UNICEF the United States ranks next to last on dimensions of child well being. Criteria include: Material well being, health and safety, educational well being, family and peer relationships, behavior and risks, and subjective well being. The United States was nearly last on virtually all these points, exception being educational well being. This gave the United States a rating of 18 on the UN scale of dimensions of child well being, with Britain last with 18.2, the only other country to score worse than the United States in the dimensions of child well being report for the industrialized world.

All the countries that scored best were in North Western Europe.

It would seem the real conditions of the United States are a far more stark picture than the current leadership in Washington would have us believe. As the dark side of the American Democratic Republic starts becoming more clear, the real question is why people would want to come here instead of their country to bear children.

Canada was significantly materially better off for their children than the United States, which scored in the below average category, in the dock with Great Britain, Ireland, Hungary and Poland, in descending order with the United States on top, well below the average.
It was calculated by:

"Percentage of children living in homes with equivalent incomes below 50% of the national median
Households without jobs
"Percentage of children in families without an employed adult
Reported deprivation
"Percentage of children reporting low family affluence
"Percentage of children reporting few educational resources
"Percentage of children reporting fewer than 10 books in the home

UNICEF ibid

It is interesting to see the conditions in the republic are rarely better than Poland or Ireland. It shows how a country that still refuses to do an official metric conversion can continually deteriorate. It is probably no accident most people who now immigrate to the New World are from the third world.

Child poverty in the United States and Britain remains above 15%. Ireland also remained above the 15% mark.

UNICEF ibid

22% of children in the United States were less than 50% of the median income rate. The United States ranked lowest in OECD countries for this child poverty indicator.

"The European Union offered its definition of poverty in 1984: the poor are those whose resources (material, cultural, and social) are so limited as to exclude them from the minimum acceptable way of life in the Member States in which they live. For practical and statistical purposes, this has usually meant drawing national poverty lines at a certain percentage of national median income.

UNICEF ibid.

Poverty in America is an epidemic, and the lives of children who have to live in these conditions, more than 15% of its children, face a struggle to achieve what their better off cousins receive. The fact that 22% of children were beneath 50%of the median income rate points to a society in need of a real programme to reduce inequality.

"In recent years, child poverty has risen in 17 out of 24 OECD countries for which data are available.

Norway is the only OECD country where child poverty can be described as very low and continuing to fall. Higher government spending on family and social benefits is associated with lower child poverty rates. No OECD country devoting 10% or more of GDP to social transfers has a child poverty rate higher than 10%. No country devoting less than 5% of GDP to social transfers has a child poverty rate of less than 15%.

UNICEF ibid

The raising of the poverty rates in these countries has a direct connection to the fall of communism in Eastern Europe. Higher government spending, often criticized and speculated on as national debt to bourgeois governments, remains a key indicator of child well being. The United States devotes less than 5% of Gross Domestic Product to family and Social programmes.

12 percent of children age 15 in the United States reported having less than 10 books in the home.

Russia reported less than 5%.

UNICEF ibid.
This figure is truly disturbing. The number of books in a home indicates the level of literacy in the family, and the lack of these are an obvious sign of ignorance. It would seem that the Ex Soviet countries, regardless of their fascination with the New World, value literacy more than the United States, and seem to be better able to provide books for the family. Thus Russia was far better off than America on this literacy rate.

The United States ranks lowest in the OECD, beneath Ireland and Poland in health and safety of children.

"Calculated by:
Components Indicators
Health at age 0-1 number of infants dying before age 1 per 1,000 births
Percentage of infants born with low birth weight (<2500g.)
Preventative health services
Percentage of children age 12 to 23 months immunized against measles, DPT, and polio
Safety
Deaths from accidents and injuries per 100,000 aged 0 - 19

UNICEF ibid.

As the fresh new additions to society it is again a tragic sign that in the American Democratic Republic children are less well off than Ireland and Poland. Given the massive industry in the republic one would think that the wealth of the country would be devoted to the children, but again we see a bourgeoisie devoted to immediate gratification of its anthropocentric adult lifestyles.

The infant mortality rate in the United States was the second highest in the OECD, with only Hungary behind it. The rate was 7 births per 100 by one year from birth. Poland was comparable to the United States, with about the same rates.

UNICEF ibid.

The infant mortality rate is a good indicator of the state of health care in a country. The number is connected with the services available to mothers of young children. In a country where the amount of dollars you have determines the status of health of your child, it should be no surprise the American Health Care system as private property would fare so badly.

8% of births in the United States were below 2500 grams, considered low birth weight. Again we find the United States on the lower end of this health indicator, well worse off than Poland, or Russia.

UNICEF ibid

The low birth weight of children indicates the impoverished and ignorant state of mothers in the republic. Poor health conditions are a main factor in this figure, as well as poverty. The poor are obviously not enjoying filet mignon at the table.

The United States did a little better off on the immunization rate, but was still behind Poland.

UNICEF ibid

The immunization rate is closely connected with government spending. It is a relief the American Democratic Republic fared as well as it did, considering the lions share of its government spending goes to war.

The United States scored second to last on accidents per 100,000 less than 19 years of age, with only New Zealand behind it.

UNICEF ibid

This is still a mystery, but seems to indicate a lack of parental concern and a dangerous environment for children are partially to blame. The use of motor vehicles other than trains and buses surely add to this disturbing figure.

The United States ranked below average in children's educational well being. Canada was remarkably better off, near the top.

Children's educational well being is calculated as follows:

"Components Indicators:
School achievement at age 15
Average achievement in reading literacy
Average achievement in mathematical literacy
Average achievement in science literacy
Beyond basics
Percentage aged 15-19 remaining in education
The transition to employment
Percentage aged 15-19 not in education, training or employment
Percentage of 15 year-olds expecting to find low-skilled work

UNICEF ibid.

The state of education in America, where parents move to the suburban areas to educate their children, is clearly not working. The two car garage and home in the suburbs is clearly a dated concept.

Educational achievement of 15 year-olds, an overview of reading, mathematical and scientific literacy:

The United States was in the lowest 5, below Hungary, and Poland, number 20 out of 25, the lowest being 25.

UNICEF ibid.

It would seem capital has less need for educated citizens in the sciences than as source of cheap labor. The state of the educational system is directly connected to the amount of government spending on programmes that promote equality. The United States appears to have less literacy for 15 year olds than Poland. Some incentive to migrate to America.

Only 75% of 15 to 19 year olds were in full or part time education in the United States.

UNICEF ibid.

This figures show a quarter of youth are not in school. One can only speculate that most are probably working, primarily for the petty bourgeoisie in restaurants serving the middle class and the bourgeois their favorite sandwiches.

Throughout all this children in the United States ranked highest in belief they would have a job that was not low skilled.

UNICEF ibid.

The really pitiful condition of the proletarian worker in America brought to light, as the children don't know how bad they have it, and expect to become the bourgeoisie. In their current condition internationally it would seem even production work would pose a challenge to them intellectually.

In peer and family relationships the United States was next to last, one fifth lower than average with only Britain lower.

"Calculated by:

Family structure
Percentage of children living in single-parent families
Percentage of children living in stepfamilies
Family relationships
Percentage of children who report eating the main meal of the day with Parents more than once a week
Percentage of children who report that parents spend time just talking to them
Peer relationships
Percentage of 11, 13 and 15 year-olds who report finding their peers kind and helpful

UNICEF ibid

These figures indicate the condition of the family and friend structure of the youth. It measures how they are living, and seems to indicate that the American Democratic Republic is having a problem providing a real leadership to its children, and that many children have but one parent.

The United States has the highest number of children living with one parent, 22%.

UNICEF ibid

It should be noted this may in no way affect the quality of a child's life, but does place a much higher burden to the single parent, likely to be a female. In many cases the right to divorce is a benefit to the mothers in abusive relationships, so this figure may not show true conditions in the republic. Unfortunately the darker side is a lack of family planning for the proletariat, under the Christian leadership of George II.

The United States has the highest percentage of children 11, 13, and 15 living in step families.

UNICEF ibid

As the majority of people in the American Democratic Republic are proletarian, this is connected to a real lack of family planning, and the quantity of messages that encourage reckless mating in the television and radio. It is hoped the proletariat in America will rise to the occasion, and reject the constant messages directed at it by the bourgeois to mate prodigiously.

35% of 15 year olds do not eat regularly with their parents in the United States.

UNICEF ibid

Where exactly are they eating? In their rooms? On their machines?

Only about 50% of American children found their peers to be kind and helpful.

UNICEF ibid

So much for the fond memories of High School, complete with a motorcar and a sweetheart.

The United States in average of behaviours and risks scores was next to last again with only Great Britain behind it.

Calculated by:
"Health behaviours
Percentage of children who eat breakfast
Percentage who eat fruit daily
Percentage physically active
Percentage overweight
Risk behaviours
Percentage of 15 year-olds who smoke
Percentage who have been drunk more than twice
Percentage who use cannabis
Percentage having sex by age 15
Percentage who use condoms
Teenage fertility rate
Experience of violence
Percentage of 11, 13 and 15 yearolds involved in fighting in last 12 months
Percentage reporting being bullied in last 2 months

UNICEF ibid.

The lack of a strong family structure and the amount of time worked by a single parent would seem to be a major cause of this risk for children. It is the last of the data we get from UNICEF.

American children were the most unhealthy of any OECD country.

UNICEF ibid.

Give us your tired huddled masses.

Less than 50 % of American children eat breakfast every day; 70 % of Russian children do. Americans were next to last on this in the OECD report.

UNICEF ibid

It points to the inability of the society to adequately feed its people. All children should eat breakfast, and if it requires the state to provide, it should not be considered to be offensive, considering a hungry stomach and work never result right.

Only 28% of American children report eating fruit daily.

UNICEF ibid.

The lack of food for the proletarian youth, in a northern country, is a dismal failure of the bourgeoisie. How they can expect their workers to turn out as healthy men to run industry is a mystery.

More than a quarter of American children report being overweight, again the worst in the OECD.

UNICEF ibid

Obviously the little bit of food these children are getting is unhealthy. In the long run these are going to be the people with high cholesterol, and heart attacks. The obvious answer is to replace McDonalds with healthy diet from the grocery store, even though it is not instant.

The United States has the highest fertility rate of 15 to 19 year olds, well above the OECD average.

UNICEF ibid.

The high fertility rate of these children is a direct impact of the poverty of American society, and the wrong messages being sent to the youth by the bourgeoisie. A constant message of romantic love being the meaning of life must be brought to a non ceremonious end, and these youth made to realize it is far better to use family planning than to simply become pregnant.

About one third of American children 11, 13, and 15 report having been bullied in the past 2 months.

Less than a quarter of 11, 13 and 15 year olds reported liking school a lot in America.

UNICEF ibid.

Our statistics end here, and the conclusion of these last two statistics are connected. High School should not be a prison, where getting beaten up daily is a reality, or you are unable to exit the premises, due to fear of criminal activity, or proletarian association.

There should be no reason adequate security should not be provided to all youth in school, without prison conditions erupting. It simply requires paid men to maintain a watch on the troubled impoverished youth, and provide real leadership.

In conclusion:

These results point to a different American Democratic Republic than portrayed to the proletariat by the media, especially in third world countries, whose children come with them to the States. Perhaps America is simply the only choice for these people.

On the other hand, if the East Europeans think America is any better off now than they were in the 80's, experience tells us the exact opposite. The dream of coming to the New World, and having a family has a dark side, and the experiences of the youth themselves displayed in the report show the real picture.

European people who wish to have children would be better off to stay in their home countries, according to this latest report. The American Democratic Republic is no longer a paradise, with market benefits to all. You either join the bourgeoisie or you don't, and even if you do your wealth is the product of another's poverty.

Thank you to the United Nations for this remarkable report, and making it available on line.

Nicholas Jay Boyes
Milwaukee Wisconsin
American Democratic Republic
3 21 2007

On Urban Trouble and Class by Nicholas Jay Boyes 10 31 06

As the trouble with the lumpen proletariat grows in America the idea of the government seems to be more penitentiaries. The class of people who make a living through drug dealing, prostitution, theft, etc., is the description of the lumpen proletariat. They differ from the proletariat in their living standards, and comprise a burden to socialist development.

As a class, they are far more likely to be placed in the military, which services capitalist society as a sort of organization that cleans up the bad habits of this class. They are likely to be forced to give up their drug dealing and usage to serve the country, and often find mates in the services that share their efforts at fixing themselves. The conservative mechanism also politicizes them into support for the bourgeoisie, especially against the labor movement. Their political economy is the pursuit of a position in the petty bourgeois, where they will take their place as small business owners, producing the various foods we eat when dining.

Their position as the lumpen proletariat is often born into. They are more likely to be the children of freed slaves, and have little prospect for labor, with the exception of the fast food restaurant, thus propelling them into the services, where they can eventually take their place in the military industrial complex.

The only real way to fix the lumpen proletariat is through labor. Efforts at industrial development i.e. passenger railroad production could be the alternative to the military services, where unfortunately, as in Vietnam, their drug habits are never cured, they just go conservative.

A steady job for the lumpen proletariat would give him the satisfaction of being a legitimate member of the neighborhood he resides in, in the urban environment. Programs for youth to learn the production techniques, i.e. metric measurements to English, could be an outlet for the trouble we see on America's streets today, where the youth are adopting a lifestyle of the lumpen proletariat. By allowing youth to drop out of school and simply find factory jobs, and support their often single mothers and her children, would be the best way to reduce the amount of their chaos.

The lumpen proletariat may never go away, even if there was full employment under a socialist government. It is a question of shifting the industrial development on the urban environment towards the inner city, instead of the suburban factories, thus the passenger railroad production example. By placing the factory in the proletarian regions of the urban environment, the desperation and lax discipline could be reversed, resulting in less uprisings and violence.

Nicholas Jay Boyes
Milwaukee Wisconsin United States
October 31 2006

On the Conflict between Christians and Muslims in Iraq By Nicholas Jay Boyes 10 27 2006

As America remains entrenched in a conflict in Iraq, the question is becoming what to do in the region to quickly end the conflict. The religious aspect of the war and the crisis that has ensued the United States since the incident in New York with the passenger aircraft has left many to question the role of the country in the war in Iraq.

Regardless of the connection to Al Quada in Iraq, the fact remains the crisis over terrorists is about religion. The grouping of terrorists with communists is totally offensive and simply not true. There is absolutely no connection between the Muslims and the socialists, and the goal of a Muslim state is not supported by socialism. The goal of the revolution remains atheist, and all parties of the proletariat support this ...

There is a conflict today about whether or not to call oneself agnostic or atheist if he does not follow any organized religion. The truth of the matter is atheist is the proper term to describe the latter. Agnostic and Atheist are all the same to those who follow the main religions i.e. Catholics.

Atheists reject the teachings of the Muslims and Christians. Religion is the opiate of the masses to all socialist people, as Marx wrote about in the 19th century.

Ones belief in a higher power in the ecosystem or elsewhere like the heavens is not even the question here. Atheist and agnostic simply mean the lack of belief in organized religion, not merely a rejection of god. It would be as naive to say we we created in gods image as to say nothing is of greater power or intelligence than the human being.

Clearly the crisis between the Christians and the Muslims has a religious bent, and the only way it will ever end now is a secular state in Iraq. Until the religion is squarely dealt with, it is an inevitable source of war.

The second way to end the war would be to give up on trying to make a profit off the oil under the ground and instead use it to help the ecosystem of the Tigris and Euphrates. The oil under the ground must be used to help the culture and ecosystem of the region, not as Chicago's antiquated automotive transport system i.e. the freeways.

The idea of going to such an ecologically unfriendly place with little or no real plan for how to fix the environment is an example of a 20th century mindset, where the environment was second to anthropocentric notions of man made by the creator in gods image. This type of idea will destroy any attempts to create a better environment or culture, and remains the bourgeois historical path of the cultural development of the last millennium. The proletariat of the 21st century, with recycling must take responsibility for the path of social development, industrially and ecologically.

The use of violence between religions is a throwback to the dark ages. It should be left to smolder out with the bourgeois ideas of production for surplus value. It is tragic to see the workers pitted against one another, who have many of the same things in common, and also the peasants, who are most victim to the past religious concepts such as Christianity and Muslim beliefs. It has no place in a socialist society, and certainly is not a reason for warfare.

Nicholas Jay Boyes
Milwaukee Wisconsin United States
October 27 2006

Chapter 3

On Ecology and the Workers Movement by Nicholas Jay Boyes 11 25 2006

It may seem obvious to some, but the question may be asked: How does the workers movement have any connection to the ecological movement? The answer is simple; its labor related. The ecological movement at a glance seems to be without technology but at a more economic level, the changes are being driven by industrial machinery that was previously not available to society. A prime example for discussion will be the Aluminum Baler.

The Aluminum Baler is a small, compact machine that takes aluminum cans and compacts them into bales, by using hydraulics and electricity to create pressure, baling the cans into 10 kilo blocks, or, in America, about 22 pound bales. It runs on electricity, and is a valuable component of any recycling operation. It requires a little electricity, and a man to put the cans in the hopper. It is hard work to fill the hopper, but it is good for the body and pleasurable after a little time on the job. Upon baling the cans into bales, the cans are put in a truck trailer, made into larger bales, banded, and sent to Indiana to the smelter. At this point they are 100% recyclable, and are made into ingots, where we leave the next processes of production to the composition industry, versus the decomposition, recycling.

To begin with the process of recycling the Aluminum Can would be impossible without the baler. It is a modern technology that is part of the development of the productive forces in hydraulics, and the electricity it runs on very much a product of the modern era. This places it in a historical epoch of production, and specifically it is in the era of production for surplus value. Thus nationalization of the industry, as was done to increase production, and using the can baler to its full productive potential, was a class struggle. It was the technology that made the change from dropping off the cans and small amounts of money being paid to the individual, to 100% recycling with the city picking up the cans that created the necessity to nationalize the industry.

In the past when people brought in their cans and money was paid for them, there were often large amounts of time the baler was not functioning. This was a waste, as an invention like the baler was totally revolutionary. There was no reason not to use it to its fullest, unleashing the raw industrial power of its glory to the international workers who use it.

Thus we see recycling is a labor intensive process, with modern machinery, and the social relationships of worker to owner, and even the desire to nationalize industry for development of the productive forces of industry. The ingots may be going to a capitalist company, but the decomposition, with the current model of the state doing the pick up from the home, and baling, places it in communism, as there is no surplus value. The lack of surplus value firmly places the social aspects of the recycling movement and its bent into both the ecological and labor movements.

Thus we see the ecological consciousness of the new millennium very labor oriented, and taking place in a given historical point in the development of the productive forces, i.e. the aluminum baler. It also takes place in a social world where the production for great amount of relative surplus value is the commonplace method for industrial development.

The ecological goal of less damage to the environment is currently only possible as a labor movement, and the development of the aluminum baler a prime example of what the labor and environmental movements can do when the class conscious proletariat and the scientific ecologist get together. They are both a product of each other equally, with the recycling impossible without the baler, and the desire to build balers ecologically driven. The historical epoch of the recycling industry is even breaking out of the framework of anthropocentric production for surplus value, a fine lesson in the connection between ecology and society.

Nicholas Jay Boyes
Milwaukee Wisconsin United States
November 25 2006

On the Iraq War 11 28 2006 by Nicholas Jay Boyes

The current conditions in Iraq are quickly deteriorating, with the Muslims in two sects, Sunni and Shiite, fighting a bloody war against one another. The American Army seems to be more supportive of the Shiites, as the previous government of Saddam Hussein, who was removed from power by the United States through warfare, was a Sunni government. The United Nations is now stating through its leader Kofi Annan the body might have to step in and restore the civil war conditions to a more peaceful society.

The addition of the United Nations, whose leader Kofi Annan stated the American led war was illegal, could mean the United States would have to stop warring in Iraq, a goal of the socialists, who like Victor Berger, first socialist congressman from Milwaukee, who did not support war in World War One, have shared with the United Nations for some time. The British have also recently stated they want to pull out by 2007.

This has to be placing the democratic republic of United States in a rather uncomfortable position. On one hand, the Americans could support the United Nations, and pull their soldiers out, or they could stay in Iraq and hope the Sunni Muslims who they loath miraculously stop fighting the Shiites. It would seem at a glance given the lack of support by Iran for the United States would preclude any cooperation between the Americans and the Shiites, but given the current bourgeois conclusion democratic republic is an alignment in itself, they may have to accept the role of the Iranians, who practice universal suffrage.

Another scene would put the Americans supporting the Shiites, as they have done up to this time, and fight the United Nations who simply want the violence to stop. The United Nations, if they were not supportive of the violence the United States war president is using, for the sake of conquering the Iraqi peasants, and the subsequent looting of the national treasures and oil resources, would be different side than the United States, who is not trying to simply support the peaceful peasants.

If there was a proletariat in Iraq it has been dormant for some time, as oil was the main heavy industry they were responsible for, as laborers. The proletariat of Iraq is left with no choice but to support the United Nations; as the Iraqi socialists are not the sects fighting, and the Muslim violence looks like a rejection of the atheists ideology, and a continuation of the old battles reminiscent of the Dark Ages...

Another possible conclusion is that Iraq would cease to be what the Americans are fighting for officially, a sovereign democratic republic. Instead it would cease to exist altogether, with the Americans dividing into 3 states, each with its own government, thus no longer a sovereign Iraq with democratic elections.

What is really needed is a clearer picture of what exactly the American role has become. We are led to believe they are trying to stop the violence lately, but as an army they are using violence, as the ultimate purpose of military movements is to conquer. Furthermore the Iraqi peasant who takes up arms most often targets the Army of Americans, or their proxy, yet it is portrayed as senseless violence.

Unless the socialists are interested in a radioactive piece of desert, contaminated by Depleted Uranium the United States used, and some oil that may still not be contaminated with enough radiation to harm a man but in a region that is in severe need of ecological restoration, an enormous task, they should support pulling the army out immediately and remain peaceful. As the news portrays all the violence as senseless already, this strategy could get the proletariat of America off the hook of having to support another capitalist adventure much like the Crusades, but with less religious connotation. This would be entirely within the boundaries of socialist thought, as the class struggle places the workers and peasants together.

Nicholas Jay Boyes
Milwaukee Wisconsin United States
November 28 2006

On Inequality in Miami 12 26 2006

In Miami, less than 150 km from Cuba, startling inequality exists. It's a if Miami was still in the middle ages, with thousands of people sleeping on the street, many just to escape winter conditions on the United States.

In a tourist economy, the presence of a large number of men pauperized by capitalism is the true state of Miami. A string of hotels line the beach in nearby Fort Lauderdale and the white sands stand in stark contrast to the large groups of workers denied even the most basic sanitation, and even food. A meal in the Miami area, if you can get through the barbed wire fence over the dumpster, consists of restaurant rejected Kentucky Fried Chicken, and water from the river. A day in Miami usually consists of sleeping under the highway bridge, where the Carbon Monoxide causes brain damage, ensuring dementia prior to ones exit, lasting for months, even years.

The only shelters cost money, ruling out the proletariat who is unlucky enough to flee the cold in a pennyless homeless condition, as Milwaukee shelters sometimes put the homeless out on the street in polar conditions. Needless to say there is no work.

It is a statement of the true position of the bourgeoisie that today the prime minister of Britain came through the airport in Miami, where he was unlucky enough to fall off the non metric airports runway, with no damage to the plane. It shows the true feelings of the party of labour towards the people once exiled and imprisoned in America, and the total disregard for the real position America's proletariat.

It is disgusting to think about the amount of money Miami Dade and Broward County bring in through tourism, where there is clearly a refugee problem, and thousands of men who, if not for the embargo, would gladly go to Cuba and reside. The ships cost money, so the homeless cannot leave, and the airport is also private property, costs money, and your not getting out.

If England truly cared about the proletariat in America, Tony Blair would visit the shelters in Miami. There he would find the real conditions of America, non metric, pauperized men who want nothing more than a hot meal and a bed. Of course, Jupiter Island, a martini, and a yacht are the closest the bourgeois prime minister will ever get to the people who inhabit the new world of America.

Nicholas Jay Boyes
Milwaukee Wisconsin United States
12 26 2006

On Labor Camps in the United States by Nicholas Jay Boyes 1 30 2007

In the United States circa 2007, there are more than 2 million people officially held in prisons or jails, penitentiaries. The rate has increased recently, and today stands at a higher rate than in the last decade. The true number of prisoners of the American Democratic Republic are unknown, but virtually every city has a mental hospital which doubles as a prison, and prison labor in its economy.

The amount of people laboring in prison, a privilege behind bars, is very large. In most prisons in Wisconsin including the city of Milwaukee prisoners are encouraged to work, and sentences are shorter for workers. The only time people are not allowed to work is if they have a medical condition.

"On December 31, 2005 --
2,193,798 prisoners were held in Federal or State prisons or in local jails -- an increase of 2.7% from yearend 2004, less than the average annual growth of 3.3% since yearend 1995.

Bureau of Justice Statistics

"Human rights organizations, as well as political and social ones, are condemning what they are calling a new form of inhumane exploitation in the United States, where they say a prison population of up to 2 million, mostly Black and Hispanic, are working for various industries for a pittance. For the tycoons who have invested in the prison industry, it has been like finding a pot of gold. They don't have to worry about strikes or paying unemployment insurance, vacations or comp time. All of their workers are full-time, and never arrive late or are absent because of family problems; moreover, if they don't like the pay of 25 cents an hour and refuse to work, they are locked up in isolation cells.

"There are approximately 2 million inmates in state, federal and private prisons throughout the country. According to California Prison Focus, "no other society in human history has imprisoned so many of its own citizens." The figures show that the United States has locked up more people than any other country: a half million more than China, which has a population five times greater than the U.S.. Statistics reveal that the United States holds 25% of the world's prison population, but only 5% of the world's people. From less than 300,000 inmates in 1972, the jail population grew to 2 million by the year 2000. In 1990 it was one million. Ten years ago there were only five private prisons in the country, with a population of 2,000 inmates; now, there are 100, with 62,000 inmates. It is expected that by the coming decade, the number will hit 360,000, according to reports.

Granma international
http://www.granma.cu/INGLES/2005/octubre/juev13/42carceles.html
The article continues..

"According to the Left Business Observer, the federal prison industry produces 100% of all military helmets, ammunition belts, bullet-proof vests, ID tags, shirts, pants, tents, bags, and canteens. Along with war supplies, prison workers supply 98% of the entire market for equipment assembly services; 93% of paints and paintbrushes; 92% of stove assembly; 46% of body armor; 36% of home appliances; 30% of headphones/microphones/speakers; and 21% of office furniture. Airplane parts, medical supplies, and much more: prisoners are even raising seeing-eye dogs for blind people.

"Who is investing? At least 37 states have legalized the contracting of prison labor by private corporations that mount their operations inside state prisons. The list of such companies contains the cream of U.S. corporate society: IBM, Boeing, Motorola, Microsoft, AT&T, Wireless, Texas Instrument, Dell, Compaq, Honeywell, Hewlett-Packard, Nortel, Lucent Technologies, 3Com, Intel, Northern Telecom, TWA, Nordstrom, Revlon, Macy's, Pierre Cardin, Target Stores, and many more.

Ibid. see above

The amount of labor camps is staggering, with virtually all prisons producing something with the labor of prisoners. In many cases it is so acceptable to have prison labor companies outside the prisons allow for prisoners to work alongside regular wage labor. Unions are the only real force that object.

Clearly the American Democratic Republic runs a large amount of labor camps, with its numbers of people in the millions. If half of the prison population worked it would be over a million people, officially.

It is odd to hear of the horrors of Soviet Socialism and its labor camps from the country with the most prisoners. An odd victory but at least the proletariat no longer hears they're doing it too.

Nicholas Jay Boyes
Milwaukee Wisconsin
American Democratic Republic
1 30 2007

On Global Warming by Nicholas Jay Boyes 2 2 2007

The totally anthropocentric nature of capital has never been more clearly felt as today when the Intergovernmental Panel on Climate Change (IPCC) released its global warming report today. Among other things its conclusions are as a result of human activities:

"Average temperatures could increase by as much as 6.4C by the end of the century if emissions continue to rise, with a rise of 4C most likely, according to the final report of an expert panel set up by the UN to study the problem.

"What a 4C(rise in temperature) will mean:

"Loss of food production:

"Droughts. African crops slump 15% to 35%. Global production falls 10%

"Increased flooding:

"Sea levels rise by up to 59cm. Bangladesh and Vietnam worst hit, along with coastal cities such as London, New York, Tokyo, Hong Kong, Calcutta and Karachi. 1.8m people at risk from coastal flooding in Britain alone

"Melting ice:

"Half the Arctic tundra at risk. Europe loses 80% of alpine glaciers. West Antarctic ice sheet and the Greenland ice sheet start to melt.

"More disease:

"Mosquitoes thrive, exposing 80 m more people to malaria in Africa; 2.5bn more exposed to dengue fever...

"Loss of land species:

"20-50% of land species threatened with extinction...

"Water shortages:

"Fresh water availability halved in southern Africa and Mediterranean...

"Hurricanes more powerful Wind strengths increasing 15-25%. Great damage to infrastructure...

Guardian 2 2 2007
http://environment.guardian.co.uk/climatechange/story/0,,2005116,00.html

Clearly the capitalist world is the culprit in the global warming, as socialism no longer is responsible for the industrialized areas of Europe.

With the failure of socialism in Europe 18 years ago the only other party that would have been responsible for the industrial activity resulting in this predicament has vanished. Whether they saw this coming is a matter of history. If they did step down due to this it was a shrewd move.

So now that the facts are in, the question becomes whether or not capital can wean itself from industry for luxurious shows of class i.e. cars, to an industry for utility like freight trains.

It seems unlikely. Capital is also unable to do the reconstruction of the land that socialism is capable of with the use of the state, and is only just starting to do the recycling. The state also provides much of the data for these findings through the space program of the United States. State ownership is the absolute antithesis to capital, and always assessed as a danger to capital.

The real changes that are required include a total change in the development of the productive forces toward ecological reconstruction by the International. All lands must be reforested, preferably with coniferous trees. Massive labor and industry will be required to transform the deserted regions to green.

Why should we transform the ecology?

Because we can.

Why did Egypt build pyramids?

Because they could.

Why did man go to the moon?

Because he could.

There are many more examples of this in history, and when the proletariat moves collectively to transform the ecology, the government and capital will follow.

It worked with recycling, and will work with ecological restoration too.

Nicholas Jay Boyes
Milwaukee Wisconsin
American Democratic Republic
2 2 2007

On Milwaukee Recycling by Nicholas Jay Boyes 2 5 2007

The advantages of recycling are startling, with far less energy and labor going into commodities like steel, aluminum, and printed materials. Since the beginning of Milwaukee's recycling program in the 1990's, the market for recycled goods has increased to the point where many materials are even exported.

"Recycling may not yet pay its own way for the 1,060 counties, cities and towns that participate in the program, but from the standpoint of the state's economy, it's a $5.7 billion business.

"That makes recycling a bigger industry than agriculture, according to a study prepared for the state Department of Commerce's Recycling Market Development Board last year. In 1997, sales of all agricultural products from the state's 65,602 farms totaled $5.6 billion, the U.S. Department of Agriculture reported.

Milwaukee Journal
Monday, April 30, 2001
http://www.findarticles.com/p/articles/mi_qn4196/is_20010430/ai_n106 95214

Given the proletarian roots of Milwaukee's recycling program, from its recycling workers, who nationalized an industry whose production was a fraction of what is it today just 30 years ago, this is a revolution created by the ecological socialists!

Larger than the states farming! The proletariat has transformed a farm economy into an industrial power, by organizing the masses to keep and recycle their waste materials.

The wonderful thing is that as recycling becomes more permanent, more Milwaukee industries are jumping the train to the revolution in recycling.

"According to the U.S. Environmental Protection Agency, about 2 million tons of magazines are produced each year in the United States, but only about 32 percent are recycled, said National Recycling Coalition Executive Director Kate Krebs.

"David Refkin, director of sustainable development at Time Inc., said "We're excited to be part of this effort to promote and increase the recycling of magazines in metro Milwaukee. This initiative ties into the primary goals of sustainable development economic and environmental sustainability and social responsibility. Metro Milwaukee will save money, and waste will be diverted from landfills and recycled into new paper products.

"Currently, paper represents about 63 percent of the residential tonnage that is recycled by the City of Milwaukee and Waukesha County.

"As far as recycling, Quad/Graphics lets nothing go to waste. The printer recycles 98 percent of all solids in its plants, including plastic, fiber, wood, metal, fluorescent light bulbs and concrete, and nearly 100 percent of all office and print-production waste. Currently, the company is installing the nation's largest paper collection system of its kind. The system, which is attached to Quad/Graphics' Sussex headquarters location, creates compressed bales of paper for recycling. Next month, Quad/Graphics will accept the Rainforest Alliance's Sustainable Standard-Setter Award for the company's role in promoting responsible management of forests for the harvesting of pulp used in the paper-making process. Quad/Graphics operates printing facilities on three continents and employs 12,000 people. Annual sales total $1.9 billion.

Quad Graphics
http://www.qg.com/whatsnew/042105.htm

As these monsters in printing become more attached to recycling, Milwaukee will continue to become an industrial power, as opposed to an agricultural and suburban county of Chicago.

Perhaps one of socialism's greatest features is its industry, i.e. the aluminum can baler is also able to be used by capitalist heavy industry, and in the future these companies like Quad Graphics are even set to make surplus value.

And there were cold warriors in the 20th century who said socialism would be a monopoly that would never be able to run factories. Indeed:

"The City of Milwaukee is recognized nationally for its innovative residential recycling program. Starting with 36,000 households in 1989, the program grew to over 190,000 households by 1995. Nearly 300,000 tons of material have been collected and recycled from Milwaukee households in the past 10 years, with 60 percent of that tonnage being paper. The City has also has active programs for composting yard trimmings and recycling other commodities including oil and oil filters, tires, antifreeze and computers. Milwaukee is also a participant in the Nike "Reuse a Shoe" program, collecting over 5,000 old athletic shoes in six months to be recycled into playground material. The City has also been recognized as a winner in the 2004 U.S. Conference of Mayor's "Cans for Cash" Challenge for its innovative public awareness program that resulted in over 559,000 pounds of cans being collected in a two week period. The City of Milwaukee received $10,000 for its recycling education program, for its efforts.

Some failure of communism! As a state 300,000 tons of materials recycled!

"Recycling businesses also paid $1 billion in annual wages to the 30,976 citizens employed in the industry, more than the 30,139 employed directly in the lumber and wood products industry

Ibid. above

Recycling has even overtaken the wood products industry in Wisconsin, a prime economic asset of people in the area.

Recycling will only continue to grow, even with capital in charge. The proletariat created the industry, and will continue to speak for it even if the goods are sold for a profit.

It is hoped Chicago, the new front for Milwaukee's revolutionary efforts will continue to expand its recycling programs, as they comprise a very large amount of resources. We should remember Milwaukee was a pioneer in recycling, and unions were also crucial, as we organized the people to bring their recyclables and they did prior to the blue can system of the city.

All proletarian people have a role to play in recycling. We have created a large industry from scratch with the help of the city state taking ownership. It has created a larger proletariat, and greatly helped the ecology. Chicago is next.

Nicholas Jay Boyes
Milwaukee Wisconsin
American Democratic Republic
2 6 2007

Chapter 4

Milwaukee Recycling by Nicholas Jay Boyes 2 12 2007

In the new millennium Milwaukee, a city north of Chicago about 150 km, is rapidly transforming itself into an industrial power rivaling that of Chicago. How was this done so quickly? How could it be this city, not a small town but a dwarf compared to the massive metropolis of what is probably the biggest city in the American Democratic Republic, achieve this new production?

The answer is recycling.

Statistics are hard to find, but:

"Each Wisconsin resident generates an average of 1,628 pounds of municipal solid waste each year, or 4.46 pounds per day, including each person's household waste and share of commercial waste. That's a lot of waste, but the good news is that Wisconsinites also recycle much of it - about 36 percent in 2000, according to the Wisconsin Waste Characterization and Management Study Update completed by Franklin Associates, LTD. That's more than double the 1990 rate of 17 percent. If yard-waste managed at home and materials burned for energy recovery are included, the percentage of household and commercial waste diverted from state landfills increases to 40.4 percent. When you add it all up, recycling more than pays for itself in Wisconsin.

http://dnr.wi.gov/org/aw/wm/recycle/
Wisconsin Department of Natural Resources

"Recycling may not yet pay its own way for the 1,060 counties, cities and towns that participate in the program, but from the standpoint of the state's economy, it's a $5.7 billion business.

Milwaukee Journal
By JO SANDIN

of the Journal Sentinel staff
Monday, April 30, 2001

Note this is a 2001 statistic, almost 7 years ago. Today recycling is way larger, but it is hard to get data.

"That makes recycling a bigger industry than agriculture, according to a study prepared for the state Department of Commerce's Recycling Market Development Board last year. In 1997, sales of all agricultural products from the state's 65,602 farms totaled $5.6 billion, the U.S. Department of Agriculture reported.

Ibid. Milwaukee Journal

Nevertheless even 6 years ago recycling had overtaken agriculture as the leading industry in the State of Wisconsin.

As a dairy state that is currently functioning satisfactory, this is a big change.

It would seem the proletariat, through organizing the masses to recycle, has turned Wisconsin into a producer of raw materials for industry, rather than a farm economy.

"Rigorous recycling efforts kept almost 1.69 million tons of material out of Wisconsin landfills and incinerators in 2000. At that rate, Wisconsin citizens could "save" landfill space equivalent to the size of an average municipal waste landfill every one and a half to two years. But such efforts are saving the state more than landfill space; they also save a great deal of energy and other resources. For example, recycling one ton of aluminum saves the energy equivalent of 2,350 gallons of gasoline, or the total amount of electricity used by a typical Wisconsin home over 10 years. Recycling paper produces 73 percent less air pollution than does manufacturing paper from virgin materials, and recycling glass cuts down on mining wastes from glass manufacturing by 80 percent.

http://dnr.wi.gov/org/aw/wm/recycle/
Wisconsin Department of Natural Resources

The energy savings are really incredible, with recycling of aluminum clearly an answer for old rust belt cities. In fact, Wisconsin is quickly becoming a steel producer through proletarian recycling.

The support of the proletariat, who started the program, and continue to support it is noted:

"Currently, every state resident has access to a community recycling program, and fully 94% of Wisconsin households report participating in these programs and 93% feel that it is worthwhile. 58% of Wisconsin households recycle at least as much as they did two years ago, and 32% are recycling more now. Over half report composting yard waste and 73% leave grass clippings on their lawns.

http://dnr.wi.gov/org/aw/wm/recycle/
Wisconsin Department of Natural Resources

With almost unanimous consent recycling has become a huge success for Wisconsin.

Chicago is just beginning to recycle, in the downtown areas first. With the addition of Chicago, Milwaukee will be in a position to become an international producer of metals, simply by using existing smelters such as Briggs and Stratton.

There are currently only a fraction of Chicago's residents recycling, but Milwaukee's example should clearly show the City of Chicago and the Chicago proletariat to continue its recycling efforts. As all that is required is organizing the workers, it would seem to be in order that Chicago came with Milwaukee into the new millennium, and join the new steel town reality.

Nicholas Jay Boyes
Milwaukee Wisconsin
American Democratic Republic
2 12 2007

On Chicago Recycling Efforts by Nicholas Jay Boyes 2 14 2007

The City of Chicago is starting to pick up recyclable materials from residential homes and the petty bourgeoisie. The cost of this is being picked up by the city, and will pay for itself, or offset the cost of this production. This means the city of Chicago will be getting market prices for the recycled goods, and in no time will be running on its own without taxpayer support. Indeed:

"How It Works

Recyclables

"If you are in one of the selected areas, you will be given a blue recycling cart to deposit recyclable materials including paper, cardboard, plastics, glass, tin, and aluminum. Material placed in the blue cart can be loose or bagged and there is no sorting needed. The material does not have to be completely clean, though it is recommended that you rinse cans and bottles for sanitary reasons in the home. Labels do not need to be removed from bottles and jars. Your blue cart will be picked up by a separate truck from the garbage and will be transported to a sorting center. At the sorting center the various materials are separated by type and then shipped to manufacturers to be used in the production of new products.

"Expansion to the targeted areas will occur over the course of seven months. The expansion schedule is as follows:
Rest of 19th Ward February 2007
Wards 5 & 8 April 2007
Wards 1 & 37 June 2007
Wards 46 & 47 August 2007

Funding

"The City of Chicago is assuming the cost of the program. Part of the cost is off set by a savings in disposal because the recycled material is not going to landfill. Additionally some cost is off set because the sorting center that accepts the recyclables pays the City by weight for the material. Additionally, the Illinois Department of Commerce and Economic Opportunity is providing assistance in the form of a four year, $8 million grant to partially fund the purchase of the carts.

City of Chicago Sanitation Department

http://egov.cityofchicago.org

The ecological benefits of this are immense, and Milwaukee's proletariat, who have already achieved separated pickup of recyclables, can attest to this. In Chicago's case, the city will sell the commodities to the yards, resulting in the city not only breaking even but with a huge surplus in no time if progress continues.

Milwaukee's recycling program has had enormous success, and Chicago's is coming along. As workers in the Recycling industry who brought Milwaukee recycling, the following methods are effective:

1) Take care of your own recyclables until you get the blue cans. There are many recycling centers in Chicago, and sorting the waste is painless.
2) Write letters and petition to members of government to pass 100% recycling laws throughout the City of Chicago.
3) Don't become overly concerned about who is in power in government, they are there to serve the people, and if enough people bring in recyclables on their own the city will respond.
4) The blue bag system is only a half step. Take responsibility for your own recycling unless you have no way of getting a car, or live in an apartment where it is difficult to recycle.
5) Get your Labor Union to recycle. Employee areas such as the cafeteria should all have recycling centers.
6) If you notice at work you are not recycling paper or cardboard, attempt to get them recycling.

These steps are what created the conditions that created Milwaukee's recycling program. The role of Greenpeace was also a large benefit. Greenpeace was able to provide literature and organize many recycling workers to nationalize the industry to promote 100% recycling.

By now, even though it has only been a short time since Chicago started their separate pickup for recyclables, they are seeing the economic benefits of this strategy, and will have a monetary incentive to continue. It still requires a push, though. It will fail without a vocal proletariat and people taking matters into their own hands and hauling the recyclables on their own to the yard.

Milwaukee's main efforts at expanding recycling should be in the direction of Chicago. As Milwaukee's biggest neighbor, the economic benefits alone should be enough to move the bourgeoisie to accept the recycling. The city should also play a role as it is good for the proletariat and the ecology to recycle.

The proletariat commends Chicago for the recent success of its recycling efforts, but we want more. All of Chicago should be recycling, and in Milwaukee it only took about 5 years to gear it up. Chicago, with more resources than Milwaukee should be able to half that. It just requires an organized proletariat.

Nicholas Jay Boyes
Milwaukee Wisconsin
American Democratic Republic
2 15 2007

On the Movement of People in the American Democratic Republic Towards the City by Nicholas Jay Boyes 2 20 2007

A rather unfortunate circumstance for the American Democratic Republic is the number of people still in the countryside, or just beginning to move into cites from the suburban or country regions. The numbers are hard to find, but the population of Wisconsin is about 4 million. Of these 4 millions, about half live in Milwaukee, the rest in smaller urban areas like Racine, Madison, etc. The rest live in the countryside, about a million.

Just what do these residents of Wisconsin do in the countryside? There is a 6 billion dollar a year farm industry, but it does not take a million people to work in the fields. The majority of these people are living in the countryside connected to the restaurant trades, small mills, and social services. They do not own livestock, or farm the land, as their ancestors who arrived in the New World once did. They instead live in the small unincorporated towns eking out a living by using the auto mobile to get to work.

It is a hard life to live away from people, and is a strange facet of the American Dream.

The movement of these people to the city is usually connected to the economic ability of these peasants to become wage labor. They bring their cars with them, and live in the sub urban environment. They are a large part of the car culture responsible for the energy use of the American Democratic Republic, and are reliant on foreign capital to bring them their oil.

Moving to the city is hard, as family and possessions, usually not large, but precious, are left behind. The cabin is left vacant, replaced by the apartment or the new home, a semi urban environment and a drive to downtown to work.

It is part of the development of the productive forces that makes these peasants and workers become redundant. If it was once the American dream to own a farm, that has been brutally replaced by the tractor, and ownership of the land by capital. Indeed, most of the land is under large company ownership, or rented to small farmer. The lions share is agribusiness, the workers more like machine labour than the old method i.e. the hoe.

Accelerating the process of industrialization through recycling, etc. could bring many of these poor peasants who live in the cabins and work in restaurants to Milwaukee. As far as the position of the proletariat, the newcomers may be greeted with suspicion, as they are willing to work for less money. Of course, under capital anyone who makes a decent living is subject to removal for an additional surplus value, as it cuts into the profit of the bourgeois to pay a full days labor for a full days work. Instead it is always the bare minimum capital pays its wage labor, which if anything works to the advantage of the urban proletariat who can live for less by for example riding the bus. Furthermore congress sets a minimum wage, as capital seems unable to adequately plan ahead for the most basic necessities of the proletariat, regardless of their bureaucratic monuments rivaling the pyramids, i.e. the Sears Tower skyscraper. Just what exactly the bourgeoisie is doing up there is still a mystery. They must be doing the mental labor of counting the surplus value gained through exploitation of wage labor.

Nevertheless the proletariat is moving into the cities, and as they do the car becomes less relevant as a means of transportation, and the energy usage of these vehicles seem to be a passing trend. Patience with the American Democratic Republic is required, as everything they came to the New World for, a piece of land to call their own, has been totally replaced by machinery and capital in the farming industry.

Nicholas Jay Boyes
Milwaukee Wisconsin
American Democratic Republic
2 20 2007

Effects of the Revolution in Cuba on Literacy Rates by Nicholas Jay Boyes 2 28 2007

Some of the gains of the revolution in Cuba have brought are not only increased production, literacy is connected to this too. It is reflected in the United Nations (UNESCO) statistics. It is interesting to see how the American Democratic Republic fares with its so called third world neighbor, revolutionary communism.

In Cuba, according to the United Nations UNESCO, 95% of girls and 97% of boys are in primary schools, with a student to teacher ratio of 10 students per teacher. This compares to an average in the Milwaukee Wisconsin United States of about 1 teacher to 27 students. In the entire US UNESCO reports: the US had a larger student to teacher ratio, 15 students to a teacher, compared to Cuba, with 10.

To a teacher, this is crucial to a child's well being in the classroom. Larger numbers of students per teacher results in a lower quality education. Cuba had a 33% lower number of students per teacher according to UNESCO.

UNESCO Institute for Statistics
2 28 2007
http://www.uis.unesco.org/profiles/EN/EDU/countryProfile_en.aspx?code=1920

http://www.uis.unesco.org/profiles/EN/EDU/countryProfile_en.aspx?code=8400

The United States had a higher fertility rate for its females, 2 per female compared to Cuba's 1.6 according to UNESCO. Higher education rates are often a reason people have less children, as they are better able to plan for siblings, and realize they are not going to be able to care for their offspring without a high standard of living. The United States, with an average adult literacy rate of 97.7%, was placed below Cuba's 99.8%, a reflection of the relationship between literacy and birth rates....

Cuba spends almost twice as much of its Gross Domestic Product on education than the Unites States. Its government also uses a greater percentage of its money on education than the United States. Literacy in Cuba is obviously one of the central goals of the revolution, and the socialist nature of its economy reflects this. Incidentally the infant mortality rate is also lower in Cuba than the United States.

The United States percentage of the number of children in secondary schools is also comparable to Cuba's, males, US 91%, females 89%, Cuba 87% of girls, 86% of boys in 2004, although if we look at 2002 the percentages are only about a percent or two different, about 85% for both countries.

It is always interesting to look at the progress of the competing social systems, especially when they are so close geographically. In seeing these literacy rates, it might be fair to consider Cuba as having reached a first world standard of living through revolutionary communism as a means to raise the standard of living of people.

What these statistics really show is communism in Cuba is not a tin pot dictatorship of the Central American variety, as the people there are literate, and support the revolution due to their literacy. They may not be as wealthy as the American Democratic republic, but Cuba seems to have made the most out of their limited resources, and created a revolutionary level of literacy in its people, and even sometimes outdoes the United States, proving than Cuba is quite literate, and understand what they are doing...

Nicholas Jay Boyes
Milwaukee Wisconsin
American Democratic Republic
2 28 2007

Chapter 5

On the English to Metric Conversion and the Ecosystem by Nicholas Jay Boyes 3 2 2007

The development of the productive forces in the American Democratic Republic is being hindered by the use of the Old World English system of measurement, i.e. miles. It makes it more difficult to export products, resulting in more labor being spent to produce parts, or a massive export industry. This is not good for the ecosystem.

When someone in Paris buys an American car from Detroit, if he has to buy a part for it he immediately puts into motion a shipping trade that is reliant on petroleum, as the part has to come from the American Democratic Republic. The petroleum has to be imported into America, requiring large amounts of labor. The burning of the fuel and the labor are environmentally damaging.

The proletariat in the republic also has to use machinery such as cars that get less Kilometers to the liter, resulting in more pollution. The bourgeoisie in Detroit to this day refuses to make cars for people who want more efficiency, instead producing i.e. Suburbans. This also is wrecking the ecosystem, and is an example of Detroit being unwilling or unable to create a less wasteful metric car.

The real solution to these car problems is to ride the bus or trains, but still to this day they are non metric transport. The train runs on the old freight lines that haven't been replaced for 50 years. Obviously they are not metric. When things aren't metric it is less efficient, as the latest machinery is not utilized, and most often it requires diesel fuel. Building an Electric Passenger train in the American Democratic Republic could greatly reduce consumption of petroleum, being much better for the environment. Even if they used coal for the electrical production at least the power plant is in Milwaukee connected to the rail yard, as opposed to the suburbs who use the nuclear power from Point Beach, and environmental disaster in the wings.

In the Recycling industry the metals Milwaukee produces could be used by internationally if the ingots were metric.

Milwaukee has the smelter at Briggs and Stratton that could be converted to kilograms, and the metal simply shipped out to places like Paris through the port. Of course, it is not only embarrassing that the ingots would be non metric, they would have to be converted and fit in to metric machinery in i.e. France, meaning more labor and less money for the same product, i.e. the ingots. It encourages the American Democratic Republic not to export ingots, as the demand is lower. A metric conversion would increase production in recycling, which would be good for the ecosystem.

Obviously a metric conversion in the American Democratic Republic would greatly help the ecosystem, through more international trading and less petroleum. The proletariat would be helped by a metric conversion, as it could increase production, where we naturally find him labouring.

Nicholas Jay Boyes
Milwaukee Wisconsin
American Democratic Republic
3 2 2007

Poland's Literacy and the End of Socialism by Nicholas Jay Boyes 3 4 2007

Poland's revolution in 1989 was the end of socialism, and the results are now beginning to come forward. The United Nations has been keeping the data on the progress of the Polish for a number of years now. It appears form the statistics Poland has had a shocking number of people who are now functionally illiterate:

According to the United Nations Human Development Reports, People lacking functional literacy skills (% age 16-65), 1994-98 was a remarkable 42.6%.

http://hdr.undp.org/reports/global/2003/indicator/cty_f_POL.html

The Share of income or consumption (%) - Richest 10% was %24.7, compared to the Share of income or consumption (%) - Poorest 10% %3.2

Ibid. UN Stats

The UN statistics show Poland has declined not improved under the bourgeoisie. Their rank is 37 on the 2006 UN report on Human Development (report checks rate of functionally literate population), compared to 35 in the 2003 period.

It should be no surprise that the growth of the bourgeoisie, in the closest of European countries to the Germans, who are currently under the Christian Democrats, is now promoting Christianity in the republic, and this territory next to Germany is now going to host a capitalist military presence with an American missile base.

Is it any surprise this was the region that contributed most to the fall of the Soviet Union with Lach Walensa's solidarity movement?

Clearly Poland is struggling under a regime of capital, as the proletariat continues to fall in literacy skills. It is hard to see as the government continues the oppression of the Poles, who were once a people who were known as the center of medieval culture.

The fall of the Soviet Union in Poland is intimately connected to the rise in rates of functionally illiterate in Poland. It appears from the UN report their education system is also doing nothing to improve this. Indeed the report even shows a large percentage enrolled in Primary and Secondary education. It is unclear what exactly their people are attempting to do there. Perhaps it is simply a place for the youth to go when the parents are working, rather than a program to increase literacy.

The proletariat must rise and educate themselves by reading and writing without the help of the education system in Poland that is obviously defunct. Libraries should be the goal of the socialists to resume the revolution there.

The International is not helped by the lack of literacy in the Polish peasant and proletarian population. Without knowledge of Marxist economics revolution will be impossible. Hopefully this is not what capitalist Poland is encouraging.

Nicholas Jay Boyes
Milwaukee Wisconsin
American Democratic Republic
3 4 2007

On Religious Organizations in the American Democratic Republic by Nicholas Jay Boyes 3 13 2007

The religious experience of the American Democratic Republic, and its importance as a movement of theology, especially as regards atheists, is one of the fixtures of society today. Appreciation of the history of the clergy, for example the role of the vita communis edicts in the 11th century, made by the pope Nicholas, are remaining a valuable lesson. Beyond this the imported religion, Christianity, plays a large role in the life and standards of the proletariat.

Considering the importation from Europe in the Inquisition of the Christian ideology, it was an anthropocentric quest for domination, with the clergy, in the priests encouraging the masses of Europe to settle the new land. Indeed, Christopher Columbus was sanctioned by the Catholic Church to search for new lands, as the church was under the king.

Upon finding the new world Christianity was used to justify the strangest of beliefs. Native scalps were sold for 25$, and African black men imported for slaves, all by the Christians. The theological connection descends from the ability of a people, especially the European Christians, to keep their ports allowing unfettered access to the slave trade, something taken for granted considering the power of these societies, i.e. Spain, who was sovereign hundreds of years prior to the Inquisition.

The ideology of the Inquisition, a Christian effort to conquer new land for the church, is yet of importance even today. George II, Angela Merkle, and Tony Blair all are driven by the ideology of the Inquisition to conquer Iraq, whose Muslim people are going to be expected to view the Christian liberators with respect as they man the helm of a new government. Freedom to be a Christian is considered a right, and the belief structure of the bourgeoisie, anthropocentric Christian imperialists fresh with this Inquisition stamp, remains a phenomenon maintaining the fact that as violent men bent on world domination by fraternal warfare between their fellow human beings, feel this is going to cleanse their souls for an eternity where they will receive all the anthropocentric needs they will have forever.

As an import from Europe one would feel this group of people would have to face the laws of the American Democratic Republic. Not so, as evidence their internment camps, open to all in Christian owned hospitals, for punishment of unorthodox behavior. It is unclear as the industry is not nationalized the real number of these unorthodox men there are, but clearly the church has a mechanism for punishing sin. The advent of modern machinery has made many Christian beliefs irrelevant, i.e. evolution and Radiocarbon Dating. Its march spells doom for the superstitious beliefs that once led to the Inquisition.. The ecological era is coming, and even the American Democratic Republic will not be able to stop it.

Nicholas Jay Boyes
Milwaukee Wisconsin
American Democratic Republic
3 13 2007

Chapter 6

On the Current State of Affairs Regarding Germany by Nicholas Jay Boyes 3 10 2007

There is much confusion regarding the current state of affairs in Germany and its relationship to the material conditions of the American Democratic Republic. There are those who would have us believe the republic is capable of standing up to the Christian Democrats under Angela Merkle, whose policies regarding wage labor, i.e. raising the retirement age from 65 to 67, are a reactionary bourgeoisie.

George Bush's groping of this leader of Germany seals his fate. Perhaps he would have done this to the Fuhrer had he been Franklin Delano Roosevelt! Unless we are to believe affection between a man and a woman has no political content, this was true reflection of the feeling of George II to Angela Merkle.

The bourgeois fantasies about the Iraq adventure being at all being like to the conditions of Germany in the Second World War, where democracy took a back seat to the struggle toward emancipation from wage labor in most of Europe are another example of George II and his ignorance or attempts to keep the proletariat ignorant.

Germany under the Christians is a bourgeoisie, and speculation on the degree of reaction after having experienced the reaction is but a rerun of the developments leading to the brutal shock of body on body between the bourgeois and its workers.

Alignment of powers and universal suffrage is unreliable as a gauge of a people's progress materially. It may have been that the system of democracy was an effective way to govern, but let us remember Socrates was killed by democracy in Athens.

Democracy as a form of political equality, that all people are given the right as equals to vote, another vision of equality, like rights given to all. Unfortunately as we all know in the American Democratic Republic rights are an abstraction, as only the bourgeois really enjoy any, and the revolutionary proletariat is left to live under the gun, and there is no independent workers party.

Germany is only trying to turn back the clock on the class struggle it inspired through ownership of private property in production. It is destined to fail, and they will again experience class trouble, as the development of the productive forces of industry under capital always produce a cast out section of society who do not own the means of production, rather they are the wage labor of capital, expendable, a cheap source of surplus value. This class, the proletariat, are the kernel of a new society, a socialist one.

The republic, perhaps the perfect form of society for the apex of capital, in the American Democratic Republic, will always include class. Attempts to create the conditions where this may cease to exist, private property, fit under the category of communism, the end of production for surplus value, in the vita communis tradition, for the proletariat in the place he dwells most of the time, the factory.

Let us remember Adolf Hitler won an election in 1936, and was appointed leader under a democratic government earlier. At the time the only other real power was socialism, and his reactionary bourgeoisie used oppression maintain its power, eventually using the Enabling Act to destroy all proletarian efforts to unseat them. It is unfortunate democracy is the justification George II, and his civil conditions in America where the communists are put down by law, especially by the paramilitary medical police, are viewed outside the American Democratic Republic as appreciation of its peoples wishes, or a reflection of democratic practices.

The fact Germany now calls its bourgeoisie the Christian Democrats and uses oppression such as raising the retirement age is only going to create class conflict. Will the German International have success in organizing a following under these conditions? You would think the workers would be atheist, or become Jews to rebuff Mrs Merkle. Of course material conditions must be improving for socialism to take root. It is only when the oppressive curtain of capitalism lifted a people attain liberation, as they are able to see another society is possible.

The American Democratic Republic of George II is never going to fight the German bourgeoisie, like Franklin Delano Roosevelt did in WW2. If it did it would only follow like the previous one, and give Germany a new bourgeoisie still against communism.

It is pitiful the proletariat would be forced to give their lives to do a cosmetic job on the European bourgeoisie. A social system is a condition of economic and political practices, and its replacement is not merely a new boss. Revolution is removing the conditions that led to the conflict to begin with, i.e. presence of an oppressed proletariat in Germany under Hitler.

It is true George II will only continue to use the troops to reinforce his vision what Iraq should believe. Until total change in society occurs, the American Democratic Republic and its parties in support of surplus value will continue, and never leave Iraq. Cosmetic change, a new bourgeoisie for the Iraqis to be exploited by is the rule of George II.....

Nicholas Jay Boyes

Milwaukee Wisconsin

American Democratic Republic

3 10 2007

On the Nazis and Ignorance by Nicholas Jay Boyes 3 17 2007

The religious background of Adolf Hitler is sometimes a bone of contention to historians and political leaders of the American Democratic Republic, who compare this leader to the leader of the Soviet Union, Joseph Stalin. These attempts to compare Nazis with Communists are completely without merit. In order to elaborate this point, let us look at Adolf Hitler's main political work that inspired millions of Western Europeans to fight against the Soviets, Mein Kampf.

"Everybody who has the right kind of feeling for his country is solemnly bound, each within his own denomination, to see to it that he is not constantly talking about the Will of God merely from the lips but that in actual fact he fulfills the Will of God and does not allow God's handiwork to be debased. For it was by the Will of God that men were made of a certain bodily shape, were given their natures and their faculties. Whoever destroys His work wages war against God's Creation and God's Will." (p.310)

Mein Kampf
Adolf Hitler

Clearly the Christian religion is evident here, as in his own words he defends Jesus Christ and the doctrine the beginning of mankind was the doing of god, as opposed to evolution. It is an example of ignorance, as the theory of evolution, even in the 20th century, was widely accepted.

"The greatness of Christianity did not arise from attempts to make compromises with those philosophical opinions of the ancient world which had some resemblance to its own doctrine, but in the unrelenting and fanatical proclamation and defence of its own teaching.

Mein Kampf
Adolf Hitler

In this passage we see it absolutely clear where these so called national socialists really stand as regards the church of Jesus Christ.

"And so I believe to-day that my conduct is in accordance with the will of the Almighty Creator. In standing guard against the Jew I am defending the handiwork of the Lord."
(p.46)

Adolf Hitler
Mein Kampf

Again we clearly see it was obviously not atheist socialism than inspired Hitler to kill the Jews, it was clearly Christianity.

.

There are many more passages like this in this book, Mein Kampf, by Adolf Hitler, but these three should suffice.

Clearly Joseph Stalin represented a more scientific approach to the political and economic questions of his day, and this led to the conquering of this Christian movement.

It is remarkable the ignorance shown by those who compare Fascism with Communism. Communism, to begin with, is atheist, and non racial. It places all men as equals, and aims at a classless society without surplus value in production. Indeed, Auschwitz was liberated by the Soviets.

By neglecting to study the real history of the 20th century we see how ignorance is used as a weapon against the proletariat. It is simply not acceptable for Christians to claim ignorance and fight communism, in hopes their ignorance catches on, or to claim innocence anymore due to ignorance.

It is sincerely hoped the proletariat is not afraid to delve onto history for the truth, even if it means reading these backwards doctrines.

Nicholas Jay Boyes
Milwaukee Wisconsin
American Democratic Republic
3 17 2007

On the Metric System in the American Democratic Republic by Nicholas Jay Boyes 3 26 2007

Probably the largest flaw in all efforts by the Democratic-Republican Congress to achieve a resounding voice of the proletariat is the lack of a strategy to attain the metric system. The war efforts especially point to a total lack of a real plan to rebuild Iraq, whose production , totally destroyed by the Air Force, now faces a Congress whose lack of support for the metric system is only going to lead to a non metric Iraq, as production in the American Democratic Republic is still in the Old English System of measurement.

Just what their intent was all the years they armed themselves to fight socialism remains a mystery. How could you talk about advancing a people without addressing their production, in the Soviet case, already metric, and therefore more advanced?

The Solidarity Movement of the people of Poland and their Democratic Representatives seem to have found support against the Soviet Union of the Communist Party by following what we call the West. Were they even aware of this glaring hole in all efforts by the Americans to create industry in the east?

The American Democratic Republicans continue to talk about democracy and capitalism in reference to Iraq. Their ideas sound fine and good, but when we look at the real things the proletariat of Iraq faces, answers are few and far between. Just what exactly are workers to do in Iraq when the only parts for non metric industry, i.e. electricity production, they currently do not even have, come from the other side of the world?

Just what the Americans thought they would do when they went to Iraq is also not clear. They seem to be manned by men who feel it is rebellious to destroy the State Dairy Farmers Cooperative, or the local Communist Party office, their own public property. Perhaps they enjoy working a 12 hour day! Rebuilding Iraq is certainly going to be difficult without metric technology, are we to think it is even going to be possible for labor standards such as the eight hour day to be implemented with 20th century industry?

The silence of the Democratic Republican Congress on even the most basic things facing the proletariat points to a front culture, reminiscent of the support for the Solidarity movement of Poland as a national culture, or the material support for the Velvet revolution, the Orange revolution, etc. or any other of the rebellion towards the working class out of the small countries most Americans don't even know the names of, or even how fast they would be traveling on their highways if they were to travel there.

The only way to fix the backwardness of the American bourgeoisie as regards the Metric system is to regiment anything under the control of Congress, i.e. State industry such as recycling, to the metric system. Obviously the captains of private property lack the will to change, and if they had to compete with a metric state factory would sink or swim. Given the current condition of the proletariat, where over 2 million are currently in labor camps, the parallel to the worst excesses of the Soviet Union are apparent. Socialism even under Soviet Bolsheviks, complete with no restaurant chefs and barren shelves might even be an advancement for many inner city workers.

Making a metric conversion as has been done by virtually every country in the world has to be the main puller of the proletariat, rendered countryless in his struggle to overcome the bourgeoisie, who has long since stopped referring to him as an American. It (a metric conversion) is the only thing that could end the backwardness of the American bourgeois, and should be a product of a Congress who change to the system and give it teeth by sending in the inspectors, regardless of the specter of communism in government regulation. Empty talk of democracy and liberty will only fall flat to the proletariat who face a struggle to produce their bread in a measurement system they barely know themselves, or have to work to understand, with no scientific basis other than the size of the Kings foot.

Nicholas Jay Boyes
Milwaukee Wisconsin
3 26 2007

On the Decline of Production in the American Democratic Republic by Nicholas Jay Boyes 3 28 2007

The development of the productive forces of industry in the American Democratic Republic i.e., freight trains, and transport, has been in decline for almost 40 years. It would seem that production must have slowed considerably in the past 50 years, pointing to a trend of production in general away from heavy industry such as railroads and ships, with only modest growth in the sectors of its auto fleet and aviation.

This suggests American production must be slowing, or totally reliant upon huge state expenditures such as highways in order to produce commodities.

See Chart 1 (pg. 82-83))

Source:
http://www.bts.gov/publications/national_transportation_statistics/html/ table_01_11.html

It is a United States Department of Transportation document I will make we have use of in this article. Please que it up and refer to it during the article.

If we are to look at class 1 freight cars used between 1960 and 2004 we see a steady decline in numbers, only partially offset by the growth of shipping company cars, whose numbers are steadily increasing. Nevertheless we see about a third less freight cars in existence in 2004 than in the past century, 1960.

This shows the decline of American heavy industry, most of which, including the railroads, are still non metric. Their decline and the fate of the proletariat in a period of industrial decline is best illustrated by the scramble to keep the surplus value increasing through oppressive measures such as the takeover of Chicago North and Western Cooperative Railroads by the largest railroad in North America, Union

Pacific. Clearly the proletariat is set back by decreasing production of heavy industry, where its numbers and strength are highest.

Oceangoing steam and motor ships (1,000 gross tons and over) have showed an enormous decline since the mid 20th century, another indicator of industrial decline. The number of these ships have fallen from 2,914 n 1960 to 286 in 2006.

Obviously without anything to ship there is no need for these large vessels, and they are but another example of the decline of an empire.

About the only thing that did grow as mentioned earlier was the automobile. It has doubled since 1960, the start of our statistics. This is primarily due to the end of the American dream of owning farmland, and is a reflection of the inability of the bourgeois to move its people into cities, another example of failing to keep pace with the current trends of industrialization that lead to the growth of the proletariat, in particular heavy industry in the hands of capital. If they were all manufactured in Detroit we could say production had increased, but a simple ride on the highway in 2007 illustrates a far different picture.

The general aviation fleet has increased by over 8,000 between 1960 and 2006.

In a country whose air travel is obviously a magnet for the worlds ragtag armies of Islam, you would think this number would have decreased after the 9 11 incident. Instead we see a general trend in the opposite direction. The Americans should not be surprised if they see more hijacking and accidents of these huge machines that are constantly tooling around the country carrying passengers.

The movement of heavy industry is intimately connected to the labor standards and class struggle of a people. The proletariat, created by the bourgeoisie as a movement of people in cities without ownership of the means of production, does not truly show itself except in times of

Number of U.S. Aircraft, Vehicles, Vessels, and Other Conveyances

	1960	1965	1970	1975
Air				
Air carrier	2,135	2,125	2,679	2,495
General aviation (active fleet)	76,549	95,442	131,743	168,475
Highway, total (registered vehicles)	74,431,800	91,739,623	111,242,295	137,912,779
Passenger car	61,671,390	75,257,588	89,243,557	106,705,934
Motorcycle	574,032	1,381,956	2,824,098	4,964,070
Other 2-axle 4-tire vehicle	N	j	14,210,591	20,418,250
Truck, single-unit 2-axle 6-tire or more	N	13,999,285	3,681,405	4,231,622
Truck, combination	11,914,249	786,510	905,082	1,130,747
Bus	272,129	314,284	377,562	462,156
Transit				
Motor bus	49,600	49,600	49,700	50,811
Light rail cars	2,856	1,549	1,262	1,061
Heavy rail cars	9,010	9,115	9,286	9,608
Trolley bus	3,826	1,453	1,050	703
Commuter rail cars and locomotives	N	N	N	N
Demand response	N	N	N	N
Other	N	N	N	N
Rail				
Class I, Freight cars	1,658,292	1,478,005	1,423,921	1,359,459
Class I, Locomotive	29,031	27,780	27,077	27,846
Nonclass I freight cars	32,104	37,164	29,787	29,407
Car companies and shippers freight cars	275,090	285,493	330,473	334,739
Amtrak, Passenger train car	N	N	N	1,913
Amtrak, Locomotive	N	N	N	355
Water				
Nonself-propelled vessels	16,777	17,033	19,377	25,515
Self-propelled vessels	6,543	6,083	6,455	6,144
Oceangoing steam and motor ships	2,914	2,391	1,579	870
Recreational boats	2,450,484	4,138,140	5,128,345	7,303,286

Source: Bureau of Transportation Statistics						
1980	1985	1990	1995	2000	2005	2006
3,808	4,678	6,083	7,411	8,055	8,225	U
211,045	210,654	198,000	188,089	217,533	224,352	221,943
161,490,159	177,133,282	193,057,376	205,427,212	225,821,241	247,421,120	250,851,833
121,600,843	127,885,193	133,700,496	128,386,775	133,621,420	136,568,083	135,399,945
5,693,940	5,444,404	4,259,462	3,897,191	4,346,068	6,227,146	6,686,147
27,875,934	37,213,863	48,274,555	65,738,322	79,084,979	95,336,839	99,124,775
4,373,784	4,593,071	4,486,981	5,023,670	5,926,030	6,395,240	6,649,337
1,416,869	1,403,266	1,708,895	1,695,751	2,096,619	2,086,759	2,169,670
528,789	593,485	626,987	685,503	746,125	807,053	821,959
59,411	64,258	58,714	67,107	75,013	82,027	(P) 83,080
1,013	717	910	1,048	1,327	1,645	(P) 1,801
9,641	9,326	10,567	10,166	10,311	11,110	(P) 11,052
823	676	610	695	652	615	(P) 609
4,500	4,035	4,982	5,164	5,498	6,392	(P) 6,403
N	14,490	16,471	29,352	33,080	41,958	(P) 43,509
N	867	1,197	2,809	5,208	(R) 7,080	(P) 8,741
1,168,114	867,070	658,902	583,486	560,154	474,839	475,415
28,094	22,548	18,835	18,812	20,028	22,779	23,732
102,161	111,086	103,527	84,724	132,448	120,195	120,688
440,552	443,530	449,832	550,717	688,194	717,211	750,404
2,128	1,854	1,863	1,722	1,894	1,186	1,191
419	291	318	313	378	258	319
31,662	33,597	31,209	31,360	33,152	32,052	32,211
7,126	7,522	8,236	8,281	8,202	8,976	8,898
849	748	635	512	461	357	286
8,577,857	9,589,483	10,996,253	11,734,710	12,782,143	12,942,414	12,746,126

industrial growth. The spur of the threat of unemployment or glorified butler service restaurant jobs keep most workers in line, and stops strikes.

The fact the American Democratic Republic cannot conquer a desert country in the Middle East also stems from this decline in factories, as they are unable to adequately fight war without supplies.

Recycling could help reverse this trend (economic difficulties), of course the bourgeois state ownership taboo is a real restriction to unfettered industrial growth in this sector. Nevertheless, the statistics show a country in decline, and its peoples misery as wage labor attest to just this. It means the standard of living is going down for most workers in America, the decline of an empire.

Nicholas Jay Boyes
Milwaukee Wisconsin
American Democratic Republic
3 28 2007

Chapter 7

On the Bicycle and Modern Conditions of Transport by Nicholas Jay Boyes 5 18 2007

The current crisis in production, the lack of a supply of oil, and the prospect of the total loss of supplies of this commodity; if the producers simply refused to ship the petroleum, places America in an unusual position. It could conform to countries like Venezuela, in the midst of a socialist revolution under Hugo Chavez, with the hopes supplies would never be cut off, and assume the workers would not learn the real use of their labor, to supply the Dan Ryan with a rush hour at 5pm every day, or it could take a more radical path.

The bicycle as a means of transport for workers is transportation par excellence. It uses no fuel other than bread, and therefore creates no global warming gases. Owned by the worker, it creates no surplus value in use, only in its production, and it is available to all people, even the most poor. It creates a healthier body, especially needed in a country with an obese population.

The path of bicycles has been given a push by Milwaukee, as lanes on the road, shared by buses, have made the commute downtown a real pleasure. The lanes have been created in many cases with little or no hardship by state industry, the road system.

Connecting to downtown with a bicycle in Milwaukee has never been easier, with the new lanes. The petroleum savings alone could easily save the money spent of maintenance of the lanes, as bicycles are petroleum free. It is a perfect example of a national industry greening itself, without surplus value.

The finest part of riding a good 10 speed bicycle is the paths, in Milwaukee by Lake Michigan, a real wonderful ecological experience in an urban environment. The waters would be happy if they could talk, as there is nothing raining down into them from simply pedaling.

Health conscious Americans, who now demand organic food, could shop in the city on bicycles, with the addition of baskets. For a small amount of money baskets can be easily fitted onto a 10 speed, resulting in a workhorse capable of carrying a variety of supplies for the home.

Bulk shopping still requires a car, but someone usually has one for getting downtown from the suburbs, or has to work in a neighborhood an older person may not be able to or want to ride the bus.

The bicycle is perfect for small loads, 10kg or less, the size of a few dinners for the family. The health effects are startling, as the body quickly adapts to the exercise, resulting in a stronger physique.

It creates no pressure for oil deals in Iraq, and for those who believe oil is connected to the violent revenge for 911 on the Iraqis by the Americans; it is the ultimate answer to the commodity useful under Iraq.

The bicycle clearly is the finest form of transportation for cities in America, as it even removes the rush hour, a source of frustration for workers. Healthy, efficient, and green, it is the prime solution for America's oil addiction.

Nicholas Jay Boyes
Milwaukee Wisconsin
American Democratic Republic
5 17 2007

On the Use of Computers by Nicholas Jay Boyes 5 19 2007

Choosing to use a computer is a large step forward for today's workers, and the purpose of the choices made by these people decide the level of creativity available to society. The succession of power from the print media in newspapers to Internet has been occurring for years now, with the clear superior technology being the web.

Computers are much more logical for the proletariat, as they save paper, the reason for the destruction of forests in Wisconsin and the rain forest in the western Rockies. The recycling of office paper in Milwaukee, and in its infancy in Chicago, is almost ready to close the loop of constant logging of the forest. The computer eliminates completely the huge Sunday paper, which was once a persons worst pollution for the day. By using the print media available on the web, a great deal of energy is saved, energy that would have otherwise been used to produce paper i.e. mechanical pulping, and the bleaching of paper, a serious cause of dioxins, the most toxic compound ever synthesized by man, measured in parts per billion.

The computer has made available alternative sources of commodities, the likes of which are unlimited in scope, from glasses frames to English shirts, where none were easily available before. With modern means of paying, i.e. credit cards, the worker faces with his connection to the web a remarkable variety of new goods to purchase, and without even a stamp and the Post to order.

The greatest contribution to society of the computer so far is the ability for communication, especially between continents and nations. The Internet allows for a letter to reach Paris from Milwaukee almost instantaneously, or a paper to be written in one country and read by another, opening the possibility for revolution like no other machine in history. The Ham radio, tightly regulated by the bourgeois, has been rendered irrelevant by the Internet, easily designed for all literate people, without the degrading Ham Radio tests, with technical questions only a graduate of a University could answer.

The Googlebot, by crawling through the massive amount of information available on the web, makes another holocaust unlikely, as governments are being required to answer instantly to the international press, and even a small labor demonstration in Europe could come up on Google news and be read in another continent i.e. Dutch Telecom workers on strike in Germany.

Non violence is also being given a push forward, as without the Iron Curtain of the Cold War, on both sides of the wall, West and East, secrecy is becoming much more difficult to maintain. For the Communist Party it means an opportunity to see how other proletarian people share the oppression they feel from their opponents, the industrial bourgeoisie. A free flow of information into and out societies reduces the chances of another 20th century approach to violence, i.e. nuclear warfare, which could destroy a whole city, regardless of even a small number of supporters of say, Russia inside the target population, resulting in a negative incentive to destroy whole cities.. As you can see, it is not even talked about being used in Iraq.

The ability to accumulate music on the web has led to an explosion of new bands, Jam Bands, Jazz, etc, who would never have been accepted by a large number of people, without the web. It allows the new music out of the hands of the bourgeois into the working population, where it sinks or swims based on ability rather than slick expensive promotion. The use of computers for publishing writings is totally revolutionary, and the best chance of maintaining free speech as yet invented. It dovetails with international communication, or is the same thing when international attention comes to bear on a website. Not only is it easy to use, after learning, it promotes literacy by getting workers writing. The pen is mightier that the sword, even a world ruled by the barrel of a gun.

It is for these reasons the socialists must attempt to make the Internet easily available to all people, especially in the industrialized countries. The ability to use a computer has become so essential to international political economy it is a tragedy to see someone struggling to obtain the web. For this end production of computers must be continued, and to keep the production in the American Democratic Republic, where the parts should be produced, nationalization must be an option. Bill Gates does not need 64 billion dollars, all this money has come from his exploitation of the working class. Regardless of his early years as an inventor, his desire to have this much capital is almost a farce. Unfortunately it is very real to a Microsoft worker, who had to create the surplus value in production that was the cause of Mr. Gates incredible amount of capital.

Workers must work collectively to help each other with computer problems, the more knowledgeable helping the less. Labor should be paid for, but in most cases the computer functions satisfactory with only small adjustments, and the Network Administrator is not needed. To this end asking a friend for help with the computer must be an acceptable way to get the thing fixed, rather than a stop at the store every month.

Computers are some of the most revolutionary technology we have been mastering yet, and if and when we do the potential for new political economy will be the highest its been in history. A triumphant beginning of a new millennium.

Nicholas Jay Boyes
Milwaukee Wisconsin
American Democratic Republic
5 19 2007

On Global Warming by Nicholas Jay Boyes 4 6 2007

The phenomenon of global warming poses a threat to all people, especially in the developing world. The greatest threat comes form loss of ecosystems that are reliant on a certain temperature, i.e. Lake trout in Lake Michigan that experience rising temperatures. This damages the ecological health of the region, as the given species gives up its place in the food chain, and its symbiotic relationships are thrown in peril, endangering whole ecosystems. Luckily it can be averted through labor, as follows:

1) Continue to expand recycling.

2) Stop using automobiles altogether except where security of the person is in question

3) Nationalize all coniferous tree planting efforts

4) Terrace all areas in cities, regardless of the private property arrangements.

The recycling efforts to date have been spectacular.

Milwaukee and the rest of Wisconsin have a proletarian recycling programme that takes care of 100% of its people, even rural peasants. This labor process saves enormous quantities of energy, and reduces petroleum through petrochemical recycling. It removes the need to mine metal, and the petroleum attached to its transport and heavy machinery. It saves tens of millions of trees every year that would otherwise have been cut down to make paper, all that have even had a visible effect, a swirling of weather systems around the Great Lakes resulting in the wettest year for Chicago since the 19th century.

The second point is more deep seated. The only reason someone downtown should have a car is if his security is threatened by a bad neighborhood for his children to ride through in the bus, or at his or her job. Health factors such as a weak constitution in the bourgeois men or a heart condition in the older people make cars a necessity. But, the fact of the matter is the bus, nationalized and in the hands of the state, remains the best winter option for the healthy proletariat. Beyond this bicycles are production of transportation that creates no petroleum, or surplus value, and they remain by far the best way to get around in summer downtown. Milwaukee has given the proletariat bicycle lanes that are safe and simple to use. This form of transit is the best hope for ending global warming.

Nationalizing all coniferous tree planting would use the state and the proletariat to create massive coniferous tree planting in all areas of the American Democratic Republic. This technique, using state money and workers is the only way ecological restoration is going to occur. Capital is a short term investment. Forest building takes lifetimes, and does not immediately produce surplus value, thus the bourgeois will never be able to undertake these types of massive work projects. Use of taxes and money saved through recycling could pay for the planting, and even individual efforts such as inner city nurseries would help. All labor should be paid for, and nationalizing the industry will start the process. Terracing all hills in downtown and its environs will increase the number of coniferous trees that have to be planted. A shift to a coniferous ecosystem in Milwaukee will give off oxygen 12 months out of the year, reducing carbon dioxide, a greenhouse gas. The terracing of the ecosystem should not be stopped by the current historical position of private property. There should be no reason why anyplace where there are hills in Milwaukee and around it that could not be improved through revolutionary landscaping, using state crews.

These changes would be a great advantage for Milwaukee proletariat, as to begin with it will create good manual labor jobs, resulting in healthy men and more biodiversity, planned for and scientifically progressed. Coniferous trees remain the plants of choice, with the White Spruce and Douglas fir prime targets for growing. All people have a role to play, and the projects of state ecological crews massive.

Why did man go to the moon? He could.

Why did man build the pyramids? He could.

Why will man fix the ecosystem? He can.

Nicholas Jay Boyes
Milwaukee Wisconsin
American Democratic Republic
4 6 2007

French Universal Suffrage by Nicholas Jay Boyes 4 22 2007

As the French go to the polls today, they face a large group of mostly men, with the exception of the socialist candidate, Segolene Royal, who all extol the virtues of capital. The main two leaders, Segolene Royal and Nicholas Sarkozy, are opposite, exposing a class division in French society, in the center of the class struggle, France.

The system of Universal Suffrage is again being tested against ignorance, as the bourgeois Sarkozy continues to ramp up the racial French heritage of the people, and Segolene Royal attempts to solve the economic problems facing France today, through socialism.

Clearly the socialists are a stronger intellectual force than the bourgeois in France, who continue to promote violence against immigrants who throw stones at the police. Their existence, a group of youth against the bourgeois trend of French society, whose unorthodox protests shook France, have created a reaction under the same man, Jean Marie Le Pen, who, with the bourgeois acceptance of the Nazis as a political force, led many workers to vote for Jacques Chirac in the last presidential election, as after the first round it became a contest between the various degrees of reaction of the French bourgeois.

Regardless of who wins this time, the democratic socialists have opened up communication with the New World, a significant victory for the proletariat. By using computers the lines of communication are more open today than they ever were before, and critiques of the bourgeois are playing a role in the political activity we see today.

For a country that previously sent many of its peasants and workers to America, the open lines of communication are a welcome to the people in the New World, as illusions and bourgeois propaganda promote an entirely different picture of what the American Democratic Republic really represents than the people who live as a proletariat in its large cities.

The election may be more of a curtain than anything else, but the presence of someone calling themselves socialist, and the uncertainty of if she will actually win, is quite interesting to a country where ignorance of economic relations is viewed as a justification for the bourgeois to continue to exploit the proletariat, namely, the United States.

Rather than care for the functionally illiterate and attempt to get this group to educate themselves, they are at best treated as a reason to have democracy and capital, a source of cheap labor to be exploited, and easy votes for the bourgeois who use racial techniques to divide them. French Universal Suffrage, used as a justification for exploitation of the proletariat by capital, rests on ignorance of economic relationships in the republic. What worker would chose to work a few extra hours for the bourgeois if he knew he wouldn't be paid? How about a few extra years, like a German retirement reform from 65 to 67?

The Democratic Socialists may cooperate with the people who show ability to lead the proletariat and speak for it, the Communist Party. The non violence is probably key, and the political economy cooperation and agreement. The outcome of today should be interesting.

Nicholas Jay Boyes
Milwaukee Wisconsin
American Democratic Republic
4 22 2007

Boris Yeltsin Dies at 76 by Nicholas Jay Boyes 4 24 2007

Boris Yeltsin died on the 23rd of April 2007, of a heart disease and a stroke. He was best remembered giving a speech from the top of a Soviet tank, the same tanks he would later use to bomb parliament, as it was dominated by the proletariat. He cut quite a figure, and was viewed as the legitimate leader of Russia by most, with the exception of the Chechens who he started a war with that lasted until 1996 and started again in 1999. It was Yeltsin who appointed the leader of Russia, Vladimir Putin, who shared his views on the place of capital in the old Soviet Union.

He liked to drink vodka, as most Russians do, but he was known to drink a little too much, and one time even grabbed a baton from a conductor of the Berlin Orchestra and tried to sing along.

His was the cause of the end of the dictatorship of the proletariat, and their ownership of the means of production.

"He was hesitant to act against crime and corruption beginning in his own administration while they sapped public faith and stunted democracy. His government's wrenching economic reforms impoverished millions of Russians poor people whose wages and pensions Yeltsin's government often went months without paying.

"In the course of the Yeltsin era, per capita income fell about 75 percent, and the nation's population fell by more than 2 million, due largely to the steep decline in public health.

Pravda 3 23 2007
http://english.pravda.ru/news/world/90276-0/

A troubling past to a leader who promised rebellious Russians more equality through Universal Suffrage. It would seem judging by Yeltsin's success in reforming Soviets the only path for the proletariat is dictatorship.

Exploitation of the ignorant worker, a practice of the bourgeois, and the violent reaction to any attempts to organize for a new society by this same group, was a practice of Yeltsin. He set up the new president, Putin, who regularly wins the elections regardless of his obvious dislike of the Russian proletariat, who has experienced no brakes on the unbridled working of a vicious market system instigated by Yeltsin.

With all due respect, it is tragic when any human being dies, even Yeltsin. But it is part of being human, to be mortal. I guess we can probably assume he is with Jesus Christ now, as he was obviously a follower.

History may judge Yeltsin in a favorable light, as having destroyed communism and restored faith in the church and democracy. Unfortunately for the proletariat, who was not the victor, this is the history that is written by the victors.

Nicholas Jay Boyes
Milwaukee Wisconsin
American Democratic Republic
4 24 2007

On Venezuelan Oil by Nicholas Jay Boyes 4 27 2007

There is a one Hugo Chavez, who in Venezuela is currently leading a socialist revolution. He was brought to power through Universal Suffrage, and is trying to build another Cuba on the mainland of South America. His country sits on massive oil resources, much of which is exported to America.

The pumping of oil from Venezuela, although it could pose a risk to the environment, is not in itself bad. What is objectionable is that the oil produced there goes to feed the 5 oclock rush hour in the American Democratic Republic, and it is bad for the environment.

The grade of fuel, unleaded, is the main culprit. Most industrial machinery in America runs on Diesel, and if Chavez really wants to help the revolution he would ship only this.

The oil under Venezuela should be used by the people to fix the forest where it has been damaged. The benefits of having a Rain Forest far outweigh any short term anthropocentric needs such as automobiles in America. Not only do human cultures exist in the forest, it is a vibrant ecosystem, the likes of which America may have known a fraction of before it was logged.

Given the choice between poverty and a rainforest, the proletariat of America have reached the point they would choose the rainforest.

Chavez should use the oil to rebuild logged areas, with terraces so the land does not erode.

Obviously the peasants and proletariat of Venezuela need to grow food, often damaging the forest, but it has been this way for thousands of years, and is not going away. This use of forest is far less damaging than clear cuts for timber, to build houses in Europe and America.

Chavez would be viewed in an entirely different light in American if he was to sink even 10% of his oil revenues into protecting and building rainforest environments. The new era, ecological, demands the forest be saved, and socialism should be the way forward. Chavez is in a position of more power than he is aware of, and he must protect the forest, and rebuild the damaged areas through a massive tree planting and terracing industry.

There will be no surplus value to be gained, as the proletariat will use the state, through land reform, and for labor, to replant the damaged areas.

In many areas the real challenge will be to protect what is already exists, the likes of which will require constant aerial and ground surveillance to protect them.

Chavez could very well become a rainforest protector by using Venezuelan oil for Venezuela, instead of simply exporting it. It is a matter of priorities, and simply mining oil is not the problem. Chavez could be the best chance environmentalists have to protect the rain forest, through socialism.

Nicholas Jay Boyes
Milwaukee Wisconsin
American Democratic Republic
4 27 2007

On the Position of the Workers in the American Democratic Republic 4 29 2007

The historical position of the workers of the American Democratic Republic is of relevance to the development of the productive forces of industry, and the changing relationship of its people to the land. The Inquisition, which also occurred in the United States vis a vis its Native American population, weighs heavy on the republic. All the barbarities, i.e. slavery of black Americans, continue to carry weight, pointing to a society experiencing the growth of a proletariat, moving into cities from the country where they previously worked the land, as peasants or slaves.

The proletariat is the segment of the population that inhabits the large cities, and works on machinery he does not control. He is viewed simply as a source of surplus value by the bourgeois who own the machinery, more like an appendage of the machine than its master. He no longer works agricultural farming professions, unless he is milling the grain, or something else that can occur in the industrial centers of modern society.

In this way he differs from the peasant, who came to the New World to work the land, and due to the development of large scale agricultural industry, i.e. the tractor, have been pushed into the cities from the countryside, ending Americas land reform programme that once gave free land to any European who cared to came and farm.

The new dream of the Americans would seem to have to revolve around industrial pursuits, such as working in a large mill, producing commodities. Otherwise we experience the oppressive reality that most of the people are definitely never going to attain the American Dream, being a member of the bourgeoisie, as someone is always going to have to work in the mill on machinery.

It points to a major shift in culture occurring in a historically defined condition, that of production for surplus value in the start of the new millennium. The profound shift in society is felt hardest by the proletariat, who have to work in the factory to survive, and the peasants who have to leave the land they have been on for generations.

The changing of the New World from a land reform experiment to an industrial culture has occurred throughout the Americas, and is a product of historical conditions of production, and made a necessity by the development of large scale industry. The growth of the proletariat is intimately tied the condition of production for surplus value, on a machine he does not control, but simply labors on. This condition defines every aspect of his life, from where he lives to the clothes he wears. It defines where his children will go to school, and whether they will be accepted into the community. It is a phenomenon of the modern world, the proletariat, whose labor creates all wealth in production.

Nicholas Jay Boyes
Milwaukee Wisconsin
American Democratic Republic
4 29 2007

On the Current Leadership and the Crisis in America Regarding Iraq 4 29 2007

In the United States, a country with declining production since the 1960's, where a metric conversion has yet to occur, the crisis of the weight of the once all powerful bourgeoisie is reaching a fevered pitch. George Bush II has committed the proletariat to fight in Iraq, a poor country in once fabled Mesopotamia, where the population could barely feed itself prior to the American invasion, with little or no wealth but archaeological treasures and a large amount of oil.

Had the bourgeoisie under George II desired to make surplus value on their adventure, the insurgency has permanently thorough warfare made this a fantasy occurring sometime in the mid millennium. The presence of tens of thousands of British men in Iraq fighting is about the only support in the world for George II, and is deeply unpopular to the proletariat of England, indicating the true state of British democracy.

It would seem it is only the wishes of the Iraqi bourgeoisie, expressed in the current governments desire to keep the Americans there fighting, that democracy is occurring. The American claim to only stay because the Iraqi government wants them there, and this to the bourgeois constitutes democracy, not the desires of the majority of their own people...

The British blatantly lied to their people, and stated they were in Iraq due to a United Nations Mandate, the likes of which were totally removed by Kofi Annan, who repeatedly called the war illegal. There has only been warnings of the deteriorating refugee and medical conditions by the United Nations recently of the 2 millions of Iraqis whose lives have been permanently changed by the imperialist invasion of the Americans, for the skyscraper bombed on 9 11, and the British and their bourgeois fantasies of United Nations Mandates.

It is pitiful to the ecological well being of the Middle East that the oil under Iraq is not slated to be used for reconstruction of the ecology, greening the desert with petroleum motors, the creation of oasis's with heavy industry, tree planting along the Tigris and Euphrates Rivers, and terracing the hills of the north. Instead it would seem in oil for food schemes the oil were destined for rush hour on the Dan Ryan at 5 pm.

Even if the country settled down and was conquered by the English speaking people, it is never going to bring home anything of use to the proletariat but perhaps more addiction to petroleum, fueling global warming. And even if the oil was exported, it would only benefit the bourgeois whose automotive culture keeps them removed physically from the inner cities, where the proletariat is most represented.
How much longer this exercise in imperialism is going to continue is uncertain, but both parties in the American Democratic republic are providing the dollars for the adventure, and the only debate is when the new government of Iraq will take over holding down the workers. The use of the United Nations for a support for the British in the form of fictitious mandates only shows the position of the island vis a vis mainland Europe, where no one seems to support the Americans or the British. It looks more like an exercise in imperialism than democracy to those of us who live on the ground in the American Democratic Republic.

Nicholas Jay Boyes
Milwaukee Wisconsin
American Democratic Republic
4 29 2007

On French Universal Suffrage by Nicholas Jay Boyes 5 7 2007

In a close contest the French have elected Nicholas Sarkozy, over Segolene Royal, in a real run for succession of the presidency. Segolene Royal, a single mother of four, represented the frustration of the socialist French with the bourgeois Chirac and his successor Sarkozy. She received 47% of the vote, with a massive 75% voter turnout, to Sarkozy's 53%.

Segolene Royal may have not won the election, but the turnout of 47% is impressive, and shows what a literate people can accomplish with appreciation for proletarian people.

The next test will be the parliamentary elections in June, where Sakozy could easily become a lame duck if the momentum of this last election proves a bellwether.

Just what democratic socialists and the communists have in common is as follows: a genuine desire to see surplus value in production removed. The means of universal suffrage is a reflection of national conditions, and obviously with the new communications available the International is reforming.

This was the first time the internet opened up Europe, and was a successful force in the continent. The loss is expected, but the message will continue to be a demonstration for change in the French Republic.

The recommendations of Segolene Royal, a more proletarian France, cannot be so easily dismissed, although change will no longer be so immediate, as if she had won.

It is time for the socialists to get back on the streets in demonstrations, the real testing ground for the proletariat, and continue to escalate the class struggle, especially with the new communications of the internet.

The proletariat of Western Europe just came really close to shaking up the system, by electing a democratic socialist. Parliamentary election come in June, and it's not time to put the brakes on revolution. The struggle is just beginning, and the connections of the proletariat between continents and old political boundaries just starting.

Nicholas Jay Boyes
Milwaukee Wisconsin
American Democratic Republic
5 7 2007

On the American Democratic Republic by Nicholas Jay Boyes 5 13 2007

In the republic, the highest form of government of capital, we see the real cause of the United States. The republic, the natural condition of the bourgeois, its historical climax, the epoch of the world market its necessity, is the true state of America. The commercial crisis of the early 90's, with the New York stock market hitting a low of the 6000's, passed into the late 20th century where the stock prices have hit all new highs. It was a direct cause of the military invading two countries, as capital flourishes under expansion of the world market.

The World Bank, an institution created and led by United States, the cause of millions of demonstrators taking to the streets in the early 2000's, has passed into a new age, where the war takes center stage. The days of the countless protests behind it, it ruthlessly pursues the goals of the American Democratic Republic in the world market. Its surplus value, interest, strikes harder than any weapon ever created by capital, creating the conditions for the expansion of private property at every deal.

Capital, sanctioned by the American Democratic Republic as a testament of civilization, the state of the world market in its climax, is only given lie to by the proletariat, whose conditions are that of maximum exploitation. The workers of the republic are not even reproducing, only immigration stops the population of the urban areas from rapid shrinkage.

The American Democratic Republic, built on elections, used by the bourgeois to sanction its world market, rests on the ignorance of the masses regarding Marxist theories, as 14% of the population, enough to easily swing a contest of universal suffrage for capital, are functionally illiterate according to its own school system, the Department of Education.

The taboo nature of all communism points to a society in fear of itself, its own workers being the enemy, shunned from all civilized culture, not allowed free association, pursued by the police informers and assessed as the latent danger of the communist party in the American Democratic Republic.

The republic, the most advanced form of bourgeois society, has reached its climax in the United States. Its flaws are only the natural flaws of a capitalist society, natural in all bourgeois culture under private property. Those who do not support it are assessed communists, and placed by default into the communist party for their representation. And even this group of sunned individuals are the main focus of capitalist efforts of infiltration, in further attempts to stop the freedom of association....

Nicholas Jay Boyes
Milwaukee Wisconsin
American Democratic Republic
5 13 2007

A Programme for the Workers by Nicholas Jay Boyes 5 16 2007

There are many recommendations for the workers of the industrial societies, and the historical position of the laborer weighs heavy on those who are called communists. A real programme for the proletariat is needed, a clarification of the goals of the International Marxists, as regards the workers. Here are several key positions of the old International, along with several of my own:

1: American industry must become metric.

2: Recycling efforts must continue, with a nationalized pick up.

3: The proletariat is primarily located in the urban centres of the American Democratic Republic. This type of culture, downtown life, is a recommendation, rather than the suburban life.

4: Production must be done for the sake of reducing mans destruction of the ecosystem, rather than simply to satisfy his anthropocentric desire for wealth.

5: All inheritance should be immediately abolished, all money going directly to the state.

6: Transportation must be nationalized, workers should ride the bus and trains, owned by the state.

7: Universal Suffrage is only effective if the functional literacy rate is above 98%. Workers must become literate, or accept a dictatorship of the proletariat.

8: Socialism must not be high flaunted goals unattainable by the average worker. Our philosophers must make socialism available to the masses.

9: Workers should live vita communis, and have no private property. Meals should be eaten communally.

10: Democratic socialists are in sometimes worth working with, dependent on national conditions.

11: All workers should be literate enough to own and use a computer, with the Internet.

12: All pristine forest areas will be protected. Logging will only occur in planted areas.

13: Small town workers shall be encouraged to migrate to cities, as the tractor has made them propertyless.

14: State subsidies must result in a percentage of ownership by the state, rather than a giveaway to private property of the workers money.

15: All national bonds shall be declared the responsibility of the capitalist government, and in the event of a change in government declared void.

16: No one should be allowed to make money off the war. All speculation in bonds must be halted.

17: An immediate end to hostilities in Iraq, and return of 100% of the soldiers.

18: Diesel or unleaded Petroleum should only be used by heavy industry, rather than the individual.

19: End nuclear weapons, by stopping mining for uranium, and nuclear power.

20: Attempt to use solar, wind and small scale hydroelectric projects to provide state power.

These are a few of my recommendations for the proletariat. As a Marxist programme this is not beyond the ability of the workers, and is a synthesis of years of revolution, combining the best ecological revolutionary and proletarian international ideas together, sort of an executive plan for the working class of the new millennium.

Nicholas Jay Boyes
Milwaukee Wisconsin
American Democratic Republic
5 16 2007

On the 9 11 Towers and their Destruction by Nicholas Jay Boyes 9 14 2007

A very interesting documentary has surfaced regarding the 9 11 two towers tragedy, brought first to my attention by Pravda, the English language Russian Daily. It is a speech by Richard Gage, an architect with the American Institute of Architects. His conclusions about the nature of the destruction of the World Trade Towers bring to light a series of startling revelations about the tragedy. It is a must see for the 49% of New Yorkers who suspect they are not being told the truth about 9 11, and the 30% of Americans, statistics Richard Gage provides us with, that also believe they are not being told the whole truth.

The documentary is on the AE911Truth.org site, a group of architects working to get out the truth about the World Trade Center destruction. Here is the url:

http://www.ae911truth.org/

On the site you will see on the left Richard Gage. Here is Part 1:

http://www.ae911truth.org/flashmov7.htm

Here is Part 2 and 3:

http://www.911blogger.com/node/10025

According to Richard Gage, there has never been a fire that brought down a steel reinforced structure prior to the two towers. This is an interesting point considering the impact of the planes striking the buildings did not cause their collapse, it merely exploded and burned for several hours. The fire is what is blamed for the falling of the towers, the first time in history fire brought down a skyscraper.

Building number 7 of the World Trade Towers fell supposedly due to structural failure that occurred from being too close to the main towers. Unfortunately the core steel supports for the building would all have to have been destroyed in order for the building to fall directly downward, contradicting the assertion the towers fell due to stress from the outside. Instead the building would have fallen sideways, as most buildings in earthquakes, etc. do.

The BBC seems to have reported Tower 7 collapsed 20 minutes before it did, and you can see on the interview the building still standing behind the reporter.

The firemen were removed from the building prior to the collapse, and how they could have known the building was coming down is questionable, as it was not that badly damaged (see the film).

Traces of Thermite were found near the towers, not naturally occurring, that could only have been from the destruction of this demolition material in the World Trade Center. Thermite is used for controlled demolition, and the finding of this leads one to the conclusion it was obviously an inside job.

Furthermore firemen reported seeing molten steel underneath the World Trade Center days after it fell. Friction cannot account for the high heat, as fire does not burn without oxygen. Thermite, on the other hand, causes the high temperatures to burn steel and aluminum, rather than smothering a fire which you would think would cool down the explosion rather than perpetuate it. The government denies this occurred.

The overwhelming evidence provided by this film clearly show a group of rag tag terrorists were in no way capable of causing the destruction of the World Trade Center. Al Qaeda as a cause of this is clearly not possible, as the buildings were high security, and it would have been impossible to set the charges without being caught in one of the buildings.

It is unclear from the evidence who bombed the World Trade Center. It is tragic because in each of the skyscrapers there were 2700 people who lost their lives.

It would be nice if we could trust our government to come out with the truth about who bombed the World Trade Center, as it was obviously not Al Qaeda and some Middle Eastern extremists. The documentaries are a real eye opener, and Richard Gage makes his point and the points mentioned quite clear.

Nicholas Jay Boyes
Milwaukee Wisconsin
American Democratic Republic
9 14 2007

**On the Economic Crisis in the United States by Nicholas Jay Boyes
9 6 2007**

As I previously wrote on the 24th of August, America is now facing an economic crisis. The foreclosures of mortgages is a precursor to the recession, and is starting to bite the working class, although the first hit were the middle class and the petty bourgeoisie. As economics today go in the world market, where borders do not always contain the trading of commodities, Europe is feeling the effects too, and to this end have issued statements regarding it:

"The west's leading economics thinktank today (September 5 2007) called for an immediate cut in US interest rates as it warned that the fallout from the housing crisis could trigger a recession in the world's leading economy.

"In an update to its half-yearly forecasts for the global economy, the Paris-based Organisation for Economic Cooperation and Development said the Federal Reserve should cut the cost of borrowing by a quarter-point and called on central banks in the Eurozone and Japan to shelve plans for higher rates.

"The OECD's chief economist, Jean-Philippe Cotis, said in an interview with Reuters that he was not predicting a recession in the US but could not rule one out either because it was impossible at present to evaluate the full cost of the crash in America's housing market.

"Recent developments have revealed serious imperfections in the functioning of US housing markets and, more broadly, in credit markets worldwide," Mr Cotis said.

"The OECD has pencilled in a sharp reduction in the pace of growth in the US in the second half of 2007.

"Our diagnosis is a slowdown. We cannot rule out a recession."

Its chief economist said central banks needed to be aware of the risks of moral hazard - bailing out institutions that had made unwise investment decisions. Wall Street is expecting the Federal Reserve to trim rates by a quarter-point to 5% when it meets later this month, but Mr Cotis said it needed to avoid giving the impression to foolhardy investors that the authorities would always be there to bail them out by cutting the cost of credit.

The Guardian (UK)
8 5 2007

The cut in interest rates to lenders is the central bank using the authority of the state to regulate the market. The last time the free market was unleashed on the housing market by the bourgeois the Savings and Loan crisis occurred, requiring massive direct cash payments to capitalists to save the industry. Today all we have left are banks.

By lowering the cost to banks burrowing money they hope to allow for surplus value to continue to be made on the housing market, by allowing for the bank to make a higher rate of interest than they would have been able too in a risky environment.

It is now hitting Europe and Japan, and expect Japan, the home of 125 year mortgages, to suffer most. A simple failure of the Japanese worker to pay back a mortgage inherited from his parents would cause serious class conflict, as having had paid 100 years for a home only to have it taken away due to failure of the worker to pay due to causes that were not his own.

The OECD could not rule out a recession, precisely what I predicted was occurring late last month. The economics are plain to see, (see my article 24th of August 2007) with supply and demand dictating the growth of the crisis.

The failure of the financial bourgeoisie is becoming more acute as the dollar loses strength, affecting the working class as a lowering of wages, in other words, a form of inflation. The solution is for the central bank to print less dollars, as this would bring the value of the dollar up again.

Otherwise the crisis will continue to grow as workers are able to purchase less commodities, as their wages do not rise in relation to the fall of the dollar. Thus we see the proletariat being hit hardest by the economic crisis in America.

There may be a problem with foolhardy investors, but given the store shelves are full it would seem to be a regular cycle, economic boom followed by recession. If there was no surplus value to be made the banks would not loan money, even to the most wealthy. The market naturally has caused this crisis, due to an aggressive pushing of the world market resulting in too many goods on the shelves, and with the lack of economic strength of the United States to consume them causing financial ruin for the bankers who predicted the military leaders of the world would triumph in Iraq easily.

Things are going to have to change in America if they are to keep control of the empire. To begin with they are going to have to produce their own commodities, with their own proletariat, or face becoming an imperialist power. To do less invites a weaker dollar, and a miserable worker.

Nicholas Jay Boyes
Milwaukee Wisconsin
American Democratic Republic
9 6 2007

Chapter 8

On the French Workers Movement by Nicholas Jay Boyes 11 15 2007

The beginnings of a mass movement to unseat Nicholas Sarkozy or make his life miserable has begun. Strikes by union labourers, in railways, Paris transit, electrical production, and artists will go into its third day today. Nuclear power workers have been disrupting electricity, dangerous places for agitating a class struggle, as they are fragile heavy industry. Nevertheless the workers must have unions, or the average labourers of France would probably never know about the real conditions inside the nuclear factories.

The disruption of the Paris transport system, an underground of biblical proportions, one of the wonders of the proletarian world, is bound to be troubling for Mr. Sarkozy. Without a working public transport system getting to work in a Parisian November day becomes very difficult…

Mr. Sarkozy has not increased the popularity of France among Americas proletariat by his recent visits to George II. His attachment to the socialist revolution of the Great Patriotic War, nominally, may seem to be the key to winning the hearts of the people. But reality is much different…

Even in the United States there remain few people who support the entire war, with the exception of the communists. Support of a few key battles such as Normandy rather than wholesale support for the entire conflict, the liberation of Russia, continue to be the real conditions of America. Joseph Stalin, the liberator of Auschwitz, revolutionary socialist icon remains a hated figure in the west…

One wonders if given the current climate of Catholic fetishists in power in France the British will be assessed as Jews or communists in the near future.

Mr. Sarkozy should accept the entire war, and not ask for sympathy from individual soldiers, rather accept the international picture. Clearly Joseph Stalin, Franklin Delano Roosevelt and Winston Churchill were together in the Great Patriotic War. One should remember France fell to the German reactionary bourgeoisie prior to liberation by the West. The Petain government rounded up the communist Jews and began genocide in camps.

It is nice to hear praise of our American grandfathers who fought in the war, but it looks more like an attempt at infiltration by the bourgeois Mr. Sarkozy. The proletariat of America wants socialism, and they are the same working class who fought in WW2. If Mr. Sarkozy wants to somehow support the revolution with his ill begotten resources, gained through production for surplus value, he should be aware of the fact without support for the entire project of the war, revolutionary socialist Europe, he is only destroying the faith of the working class in his reform school tactics at home.

One thing that is clear in the movement of the French proletariat is its numbers are small, but in the right places.. Unfortunately it will be difficult to maintain, as only 1 in 10 workers in France are in a union. It is this fact which makes the strikes so captivating, can a small number of labourers in heavy industry affect French society?

The only reason French workers at some point in the future would have to work more than thirty five hours a week would be to shift the industry away from nuclear power. The Sarkozy government is not proposing this. This will come painfully later in history when the inevitable accident in a too heavily reliant on nuclear power bourgeois society occurs, accidental of course. Averting this must come from those workers who are today disrupting power in France from the stations, without violence in the plants.

Perhaps Mr. Sarkozy's real desire is to use America as a prison colony again as the French once did in New Orleans. Given the one way traffic of the fall of the Berlin Wall, with America like a big Hotel California, the real motion of the bourgeoisie of Western Europe, it would be very convenient at the moment. France could send its workers in exile to

America where they would work longer hours, have less disposable income, not be metric, all the treatments of a prisoners. England could chime in with the immigrant problem they have been facing for a number of years. Simply send them all to the land of the free market, the land of the free trade!

The French are reaching a defining moment in history, whether or not they decide to support the revolution, and accept all powers in the last war, or if they will continue to support only Britain and America. It is a trying time, but bold decisive leadership on the part of the French union movement could change French society.

Nicholas Jay Boyes
Milwaukee Wisconsin
American Democratic Republic
11 15 2007

On the French Labour Movement by Nicholas Jay Boyes 11 17 2007

The strike in France is in its fifth day, with the unions continuing to demonstrate against Sarkozy and his reform school tactics. Clearly the railroad industry, already nationalized, will not submit to the free market strategies of the new Prime Minister.

On Tuesday many more workers will be joining the strike, just about three days away. It looks like the railroad workers, who have halted much of the passenger railroad system in Paris and the rest of France, will stick it out another 3 days, the result of which will be a large strike against Nicholas Sarkozy.

Most of the press seems to be focused on the number of workers who went to work anyhow, but there are still many of the 500,000 workers affected by Sarkozy's efforts to increase surplus value through raising the retirement age on strike. He is also attempting to raise absolute surplus value through ending the 35 hour workweek, a typical tactic of producers of capital.

Thus it is no surprise the proletariat is dismayed at the turn the new government of the prime minister has taken. Chirac, in 1995 also tried to erode the rights of labourers, but was forced to climb down when the workers clearly would not have it.

France of the 19th century was the center of the class struggle, site of the first communist revolution, the Paris Commune. It was short lived, but the proletariat there laid down the plans for the new socialist society, and was influential in Russia at the beginning of the Soviet Union.

By the 20th century Germany becomes more dominant in the class struggle, with the reactionary bourgeoisie of Adolf Hitler becoming very territorial and attacking the Russian revolution. The communist movement of the workers clearly caused frustration with the bourgeoisie, resulting in the fury of battle coming from the German leadership. The battle was won, and half of Germany became socialist, placing it in the center of the movement.

With the change in government in the Soviet Union, and the end of socialism in the east, France again is becoming the center of the struggle. It is becoming clear the Russian people are scared to death of communism, and trust leaders like Sarkozy. It would seem many Eastern Europeans listen to AM radio for their news, much the same as the early 20th century, when Poland was a capitalist country. Their attachment to antiquated means of communication defines the attempts to roll back the wheel of history, and to restore the bourgeoisie to power in the East of Europe.

So the historical context of the strike is that of a general breakdown of the rights of workers in Europe, the division of labour and the bourgeoisie, both asserting dominance in the western regions of the continent. Sarkozy may be the face of the new Europe, nominally in favor of the socialist revolution of the last war, but sticking to capitalism in practice. Obviously he is attempting to dismantle the rights of labourers, and has offended the labourer clearly showing his bourgeois nature....

Like America, the French passenger railroad is nationalized, and run by the French state as SNCF, in America called Amtrak. The ability to run the national railroad rests on the unionized labourers, who perform all the manual labour. Neither system produces surplus value, although there are bonds issued for the state in America, which create surplus value through speculation on the states debts, always increased when a conservative government takes power, i.e. George II. Thus the bourgeoisie even finds ways to make money off the state, nationalized industry...

Sarkozy's Union for a Popular Movement (UMP) party certainly seems only popular with the bourgeoisie, and the numbers of strikers who will be going to the picket lines come Tuesday will numerically outnumber his soon. With the stoppages costing an estimated 600 million dollars a day, Sarkozy must feel very popular indeed...

One thing this type of activity shows is contrary to the picture we are shown by Hollywood of working class life being boring is simply not true. There is no shortage of entertainment in the revolution, and the

123

proletariat is the driver. Expect more excitement come Tuesday, when many more workers join the movement.

Nicholas Jay Boyes
Milwaukee Wisconsin
American Democratic Republic
11 17 2007

On the French Strike of 11 20 2007 by Nicholas Jay Boyes

"SCHOOLS closed, flights delayed, trains cancelled and newspapers not printed - that was the picture in France yesterday, as civil servants joined transport workers in strikes to challenge President Nicolas Sarkozy's reform programme."

Scotsman
10 20 2007

"Public sector employees – including teachers, air-traffic controllers, nurses postmen, street cleaners, refuse collectors and junior civil servants – were among those who staged a one-day stoppage yesterday in protest against plans for cuts in public sector jobs and the erosion of their standard of living by seven years of low pay rises. The eight trades union federations claimed that about half the 2.5 million state sector workers had joined the strike…

Independent (UK)
10 20 2007

Clearly the numbers speak for themselves, with millions of workers striking against a "popular" Sarkozy. One wonders what exactly is considered "unpopular" in France!

The forces of change are sweeping France, and the proletariat is clearly making itself felt on the streets. The bourgeoisie of France is appealing for calm and an end to the protests, which could come for some of the segments of the working class, whose goal was a day or two of demonstrations. Unfortunately for Mr. Sarkozy his trouble with the railway workers is probably not going away for some time, even if the workers return to work.

It is often hard to gauge the true feelings of a people for its leaders, a bourgeoisie in France, in this case. The system of voting is not always the best method for seeing the true feelings of a people, as it is easily dominated by the so called "betters" of the labourer. Thus we see the true feelings of the French not expressed in the elections, and rather we look from America to the streets, much like conditions here on the other side of the Atlantic in the New World, when looking for the real conditions of a people.

The demonstrations in France show the worker will not be taken by promises of freedom from Mr. Sarkozy, meant by him free trade, free markets. Apparently the drive to increase surplus value by the bourgeoisie is meeting resistance in France, and we can see it today with our new machinery, the Internet.

With the number of workers on strike one would think Mr. Sarkozy would back down, and stop trying to increase relative surplus value by lengthening the workweek. Instead we see the "popular" leader looking like and American hard liner, vowing to stay on until the end of his term, regardless of public opinion.

Do not be fooled, there is much for the French proletariat to gain from striking. Now we see the hand of the bourgeoisie, with Sarkozy on the defensive. The American proletariat sees the French struggle, and segments of the working class are bound to support it. As an exile population from Europe we understand all too clearly the frustration and feelings of isolation, but do not be dismayed, your message is clear. No increasing the absolute surplus value by the bourgeoisie!

Nicholas Jay Boyes

Milwaukee Wisconsin

American Democratic Republic

11 20 2007

On Conditions in Russia by Nicholas Jay Boyes 11 26 2007

With elections only about a week off in Russia, it is a good time to reflect on what exactly this process has brought to the people of this large country. The first thing that occurred due to the end of the dictatorship of the proletariat, which had been disintegrating from the time of Joseph Stalin's death, as the growth of a bourgeoisie. It is sad but it would seem the people of Russia were taken by dreams of material wealth, and the desire to allow for some people to have more wealth than others as opposed to equality.

This movement toward private property caused the end of the Soviet Union. As the bloc fell, all countries whose once Communist Party governments were made to have elections experienced a rapid growth of the bourgeoisie in the parties vying for power in the now democratic countries.

For some people the fall of communism meant a better standard of living, but it was at the expense of the proletariat. Weakening of the workers state caused the less read to spend their time in attempts at self gain, as opposed to recognition of their membership in the working class.

As the workers state broke down due to the influence of the new elected leaders the inequality rose phenomenally. The industry once created and controlled by the proletariat was mercilessly removed from their hands, and placed under a bourgeoisie. The material gains may have been good, but a collective consciousness of the common plight of the peasant and worker and its dignity was removed, and the base self interest returned with a vengeance.

As the millennium turned the ecological consciousness began to grow in Russia, as with all industrialized society. Unfortunately it was not finding fertile ground, as the bourgeoisie was threatened by the movement, and continued to attempt to remove the industry from the hands of the people most affected by the industrial pollution, the proletariat. Thus little was done to promote a cleaner environment, and nuclear power for example was still used, only now for the bourgeoisie.

It would seem the elections were only used long enough to create a bourgeoisie, as by the time 2007 came the OSCE was no longer monitoring elections on Russia. The democratic period of Russian history effectively came to an end, after a mighty empire of the proletariat brought to its knees, and left with an oligarchy opposed to the interests of the workers.

It is a tragic tale, and shows the ability of the bourgeoisie of Western Europe and America to influence people to do just about anything for wealth and power. At the end of the democratic period, once considered a freedom for the Russian people, we are left with a country in shambles, totally ravaged by unbridled free market economics for 20 years, with homelessness returning, prostitution, etc.

The Kommunist Party of the Russian Federation is predicted to gain a small number of seats in the parliament after the elections on the 2nd. It is not clear if the Party is even seriously attempting to run in the elections, as they often see the elections as an opportunity to weaken socialism. It is unfortunate but people are too easily able to manipulate the elections by promising wealth and power to followers of the parties of the bourgeoisie. Material advantages of capitalism are hardly worth the damage they do to the ecology, i.e. cars and global warming. The same is true towards society of men if to enjoy luxuries creates an impoverished worker…

The total lack of a collective consciousness on the part of the people who believe they are better off with capitalism is pitiful. They do not see the international movement of the labourer, and if confronted by the labourer demanding an end to surplus value, nationalization of industry, either do not understand their goals or must feel they are being lied too by the proletariat.

Unfortunately having been taken so many times in the past, lately by the pro democratic leadership of Russia, who point to increases in the standard of living of the average person without regard for the real social and ecological cost of the production, many people are apathetic to the reality even when shown the truth.

A position as opposition in the parliament by the KPRF may create more favorable conditions for the labourer, but voting will also strengthen the bourgeoisie under Putin, whose past activities under Yeltsin included bold faced expropriation of worker property with a meager compensation, will be able to say they legitimately took power. Perhaps the OSCE is not the only group who should be stopping participation in Russian elections....

Nicholas Jay Boyes
Milwaukee Wisconsin
American Democratic Republic
11 26 2007

On International Recycling by Nicholas Jay Boyes 11 27 2007

The main problem facing Russia today, in the large cities, would seem to be a lack of recycling. Information is difficult to come by, most of it is either in a language few here understand, or is simply not available. What we do know is Russia is still primarily using integrated steel production techniques, as opposed to electric arc furnace technology. In other words, they are mining iron and smelting it as opposed to recycling it, virgin steel vs. scrap.

It would seem many regions of America i.e. Chicago are in the same boat. Chicago is just starting to recycle, with many areas of the metropolis still without a state pickup. Integrated steel production is still being used, with United States Steel one of the forces of production.

Thus one could say America was in no position to suggest Russia recycle. Fortunately, there are cities and regions such as Milwaukee and Wisconsin, North of Chicago, who have been recycling for about ten years now, with a state pickup at the street.

Thanks to these efforts more than half of United States steel production occurs in the electric arc furnace. It is a real accomplishment, and far less damaging to the ecology than mining the earth.

Thus we return to Russia. Russia is starting again to look to the old Soviet technology, much of it expropriated from the proletariat by the Yeltsin- Putin cliché. The amount of production is still impressive, but could be greatly helped if the government there was to start a recycling programme.

"Evraz posted a first-half net profit of $1.13 billion, the highest among Russia's big four steel makers for the period, after becoming the world's largest rail producer through its purchase of Oregon Steel Mills in the United States.

"Evraz is Russia's largest steel maker by domestic volume. Rivals Novolipetsk posted first-half net profit of $1.07 billion, Severstal $999 million and Magnitogorsk Iron and Steel Works $866 million.

130

"Evraz's main shareholders include Frolov, Alexander Abramov and Russia's richest man, Roman Abramovich, whose investment vehicle last year acquired a 41 percent stake in the company.

Reuters 10 5 2007

Obviously the bourgeoisie is still functioning inside Russian steel, created again by the Putin – Yelsin cliché. The presence of large amounts of surplus value leads one to wonder if production by this method is outdated, as in America production of integrated steel mills is often not metric, as the machinery is old.

Simple rejection of the old production techniques and a change to electric arc furnaces would seem to be the logical solution. Why even try to fix an old integrated mill?

The amount of surplus value created by the integrated mill process is probably larger in America than in Russia, as the bourgeoisie is more entrenched.

It basically is senseless to attempt to create socialism at an American integrated mill, as it is not even metric. In Russia it is 20th century industry. Thus recycling is the path of the proletariat that must be followed, with a state pickup and the electric arc furnace.

The integrated mill conditions are that of an anthropocentric vision of the world, of human need before ecology. The electric arc furnace technology is the complete opposite, as it takes what was once a waste product, steel scrap and cans, and turns it into a useful steel product, ingots.

Thus the more than half of American steel production is in electric arc furnaces…

Given the fact Putin seems not to be moving from power, the proletariat of Russia should demand Putin create a recycling programme, in the large cities of the west such as St. Petersburg and Moscow. It shouldn't have to be a concession either, as it is simply logical.

A state pickup is a necessity, and there is no reason why Milwaukee's successes should not be useful to the proletariat of Russia. In Milwaukee the state sells the recyclables to the market people, and makes good money. Moscow could follow…

Russia is clearly not going to change leadership December second, so it would be a good time to figure out how get it out of Putin to help the proletariat. There is no reason why recycling should be a monopoly of the west, when it is obviously not a secret, a change done by nationalization.

Nicholas Jay Boyes
Milwaukee Wisconsin
American Democratic Republic

11 28 2007

On Dialectical Materialism and Industry by Nicholas Jay Boyes 12 29 2007

The nature of mans thought is grounded in language, primarily developed to adapt to material conditions. It may be possible to think in images, especially artistic i.e. musical scores, etc., but to learn technique, in this case musical theory, requires language.

When discussing matters of a philosophical or political economic nature the language is the method by which man thinks. It is inherently social, and the meanings of the language of words rooted in the material conditions man finds around him.

Dialectical materialism places mans thought in the realm of the social, the theory being the level of the development of the productive forces of industry historically govern the ability of man to communicate and think.

Indeed, the number of new words to describe industrial natural scientific developments probably easily outnumber that of any political economy or philosophy language.

This is not to say that the lack of words is a restriction, rather to point out the number of words to describe i.e. a motor and its parts are simply greater in number than, for instance social class in society.

The development of language and the number of its words are obviously in this respect a direct adaptation to the material conditions of production that man finds himself historically.

As the class struggle escalates the modern conditions create a more pitched battle, with the new dialect reflecting the changing material conditions, and adaptation to the exploitation of the proletariat for production for a greater amount for relative surplus value by his so called betters.

The class conflict brings forth new conditions in the modern world daily, especially for the proletariat who directly experiences the natural world when labouring.

Everything social we know is rooted in language, musical notes another form of language. It is a social phenomenon, created by man over the long ages since the development of language....

It is very much an ecological phenomenon as well, as new knowledge of the natural world brings forth new ideas, rooted in language defined by the changing awareness of mankind's relationship to the natural world.

As material things are but an inanimate extension of self, the ecological consciousness of man is inherently connected to the ecology. Modern mans ecology is simply more conditioned by the products of labour, which all stem from the relationship of man to ecology.

A clean indoor environment is in many ways a clean outdoor one, with a few notable exceptions such as dishwashers, for example, which use too much energy. Fortunately, for the ecology, energy efficiency is the new culture of the proletariat, and even the big cars of the past i.e. limousines are becoming the dinosaurs of the 20th century. And who wouldn't rather ride a bicycle on a fine spring morning than drive a car to get downtown?

The language and dialect of a people are rooted in their material conditions, and the ecological movement is also a historical development of industry, to communicate, i.e. the internet, the ability to recycle. The dialect and thought of mankind is also shifting towards ecological socialism, as new inventions continue to change the anthropocentric thought of the past.

The internet has brought us out of the modern era, and is placing us in the ecological era. The days are gone when any government, even the

American Democratic Republic could restrict communication between fellow exploited workers. This revolutionary technology is the latest example of industry shaking the very foundations of society. The potential for revolution has never been greater...

Nicholas Jay Boyes
Milwaukee Wisconsin
American Democratic Republic
12 29 2007

**On the Development of the Productive Forces to Create Private
Property and its Effects by Nicholas Jay Boyes 12 4 2007**

By the dawn of the new millennium the failure of the development of
the productive forces of industry in the direction of private property was
clearly visible. The engineering projects of the 20th century, Cars on the
Autobahn Superhighway, for example, were destroying the ecosystem.
Many other components of the modern bourgeois state were failing as
well, jet aircraft and missile technology, all engineered by the Germans
in the reactionary bourgeois period.

The failure of the industrial model of Germany, the Autobahns, for
instance, points to a total failure of the bourgeoisie to plan ahead for the
coming shift away from anthropocentric industry to ecological industry.

Given the level of development of the Germans, whose industry at first
conquered most of Europe under the reactionary bourgeoisie of Adolf
Hitler, and then later was adopted by the European people in the West in
particular, shows the disregard of anthropocentric bourgeois culture to
see beyond the desire for private property in the life of the individual.

So many of the hallmarks of bourgeois society, trips on jets, fast cars,
missile defense systems, all created an ecological and social crisis. The
development of missiles by the United States with Nazi engineers after
the Second World War was a complete failure, and did not improve the
security of the people against a reactionary bourgeoisie at all. In fact it
was suicidal, as it created an arms race between the Communist Party of
Russia and the United States, the likes of which miraculously never
resulted on all out war. Hitler's dream of the rejection of communism by
the Allied Powers came true, and it was due to the development of the
industrial productive forces all created by the reactionary bourgeoisie
under Adolf Hitler.

Cars became the producers of global warming gases, raising the
temperature of the Earth several degrees, melting the polar icepacks,
threatening extinction of Polar Bears, and raising the level of water of
the oceans. Social and economic chaos followed, and the personal
private property of the automobile was the main cause. The

Superhighway was the culprit, otherwise known as the Autobahn, an invention of the reactionary bourgeoisie of Adolf Hitler.

Jet aircraft became a major component of bourgeois warfare, with the violent conquering of the proletariat by jet aircraft in the Soviet Union a plan hatched by the owners of private property, another of Hitler's dreams.

Nuclear missiles, based of the same technology of the Nazis that bombed London in the 40's, created by the same engineers in America, transplanted from Germany to the United States for the American bourgeoisie, practically caused a nuclear war between the same powers who had cooperated previously, the Soviets and the Americans, another achievement of the German reactionary bourgeoisie.

The ecological cost of these creations of the German bourgeoisie were very detrimental to social and ecological progress in the new millennium, and there was no way to just go back to the old way of doing things once the industry for private property was unleashed. Aircraft were the ultimate form of capital, by necessity movable property, as opposed to railroad tracks. They offered a mechanism to keep down the proletariat by stopping strikes on railroad tracks, the other form of passenger travel, and shipping ports, another form of immovable property thus vulnerable to strikes.

The addiction of the bourgeoisie to this type of idea, industry to oppress the labourer, was the cause of the ecological collapse of the new millennium, and led to the rejection of these types of industry by the ecological era proletariat.

The bourgeoisie was falling on its own weight, with the ecological and social crisis all their own doing bringing them down. The petroleum to fuel the cars ran out in America prior to the new millennium, and had to be shipped from across the ocean, causing oil spills and air pollution. It was clearly unsustainable, and the Autobahn Superhighway the main user of petroleum.

Nuclear missile technology, like all industry, was not kept secret for long, and soon even Pakistan had the bomb. The missile was the vehicle of delivery, created by the Nazis in the last millennium.

It continues today and he only way to root out this fascination with reactionary bourgeois industry is revolutionary ecological socialism. The production for surplus value creates conditions that lead to the bourgeoisie constantly attempting to drag down the labourer, to have to own a car, for instance, social needs created by adoption of the reactionary bourgeois industry.

Until the labourer controls the means of production, the ecological crisis will never go away, it will only get worse. Nationalized passenger and freight railroads are the mechanism to correct the transit problem, as they are very efficient even with diesel. But they also are magnets for union activity, requiring communism.

Rejection of jet aircraft is yet to come, but it is an obvious cause of air pollution, as it is up there burning jet fuel and reaching the upper layers of the atmosphere. A shift to ships and railroads is in order, that do not pollute the upper atmosphere.

Missile production is suicidal, a hallmark of the anthropocentric society of the 20th century, a tool of the reactionary bourgeoisie. The Soviet Socialists recognized this in the 20th century, and gave up their missiles. It is surprising they were fooled for as long as they were…

The ecological era is shifting society in a proletarian direction, and the bourgeoisie is falling on its own weight. Unless they change their industrial activity they are irreparably going to destroy the ecology, and even now they are generally viewed with distrust when adopting their private property in the community.

The reactionary bourgeoisie was a historical phenomenon of the last millennium, whose technology was far more logical then than now. Anthropocentric industry was the rule, and it has been shaken by the ecologists in the new millennium. It must now sink or swim in the new ecological era...

Nicholas Jay Boyes
Milwaukee Wisconsin
American Democratic Republic
12 4 2007

On Economic Conditions in the United States by Nicholas Jay Boyes 12 8 2007

The quality of life in America has been in decline for years now, with the deindustrialization of many cities leading to crisis. America now faces tough choices, with the current escalation of the economic crisis, in particular in the home mortgage market.

The failure to build industrial production, the shift to a distribution based economy, reliant on cheap imports from the less industrialized countries is playing a part in the crisis. By shifting unionized production to the third world the people who used to be able to do things like buy homes is decreasing, and the free trade agreements that were supposed to move capital into the United States failing due to nationalization in the countries that were being exploited as a source of cheap labour.

Venezuela and Iran have both nationalized their petroleum production, and Iraqi oil is not currently available. This has risen the price of oil considerably, requiring more labour to produce commodities. With the current modern conditions of production, heavily reliant on petroleum to run factories, and the materials for petrochemicals i.e. plastics, the rise in cost has struck the housing market first. Simply put, without a plan to replace the factories removed by the bourgeoisie, who thought they could make more surplus value in foreign countries with their capital than in the United States, and subsequently moved production to the third world, now face a reality: the workers can no longer afford the products they produce, and the dream of home ownership is beginning to fade for the proletariat.

It is inevitable that without imperialist free trade, currently going out of style, the mother country of the industries currently outside it must suffer. The entire purpose of moving capital to the developing world, the quest for increased surplus value, rests on an exploited labourer. Given the fact the labourer in the developing world is asked to accept greater inequality than in the industrialized world, naturally nationalization of industry becomes easier in the countries affected by imperialism. Thus we have a Hugo Chavez, who is nationalizing petroleum in Venezuela, raising the price of oil and thus the price of commodities created with it in America.

Nationalization is not completely to blame though. The contraction of the economy is also created by the enormous sums being spent to fight war in Iraq, a war that is proving to be unprofitable. The only real wealth in Iraq is petroleum, and in order to rebuild after the destruction 5 years of all out war have caused it is questionable if the American bourgeoisie will ever be able to make the Iraq war a surplus value creator...

It is interesting the crunch is starting to be seen in the housing markets, as this is sort of a petty bourgeois and middle class domain. The proletariat has suffered from the deindustrialization of America for years, faced with no skills even to work in a foreign company, as he has to be retrained to use the metric system, since all American factories are still not metric.

The middle class wields considerable weight, as they are the favored class by the bourgeoisie. Whenever it is time for bourgeois democracy, the successes of the middle class and petty bourgeoisie to live well are always pointed too.

The conditions of the proletariat in America have been declining for decades, as heavy industry that is not metric is not competitive on the world market, resulting in shuttered factories in the rust belt. Every industry removed from a city causes poverty, and this desperation of poverty creates the conditions for urban violence and a larger lumpen proletariat.

Jobs in distribution, Wal Mart, etc. do not create nearly as much money for the labourer as production. This is not all due to the miserliness of the distribution bourgeoisie, it is a product of the lack of skill required to sell commodities on the store shelf. The skilled worker is not present at Wal Mart, and the products sold are sold at the lowest price possible. To remain competitive the wages are low, the commodities often produced in the third world.

A unionized distribution facility would not change the production structure of American society. The surplus value is already in the commodity when reaching distribution, and when it reaches retail the surplus value from retail sales small. All attempts to control production through distribution are bound to fail, as competition regulates the market, and the cheaper commodity will always be the one that sells…

The only way out of the crisis is to make a metric conversion, and reindustrialize America with clean heavy industry i.e. recycling. The nationalization of industry must be addressed, with the newer heavy industries where need is most pressing, a pickup of recyclables nationwide by the state.

Without a concrete plan for a metric conversion American conditions are going to continue to decline, as nobody wants to buy a non metric product compared to a metric one. The latest economic crisis shows again the failure of the bourgeoisie to move forward out of 20th century production techniques, non metric industry, to the 21st century, green metric technology. The production techniques connected to warring for surplus value are also failing, as the industrial failure of non metric industry has lowered the ability for the army to fight by modern standards, resulting in the Iraq disaster. The mortgage crisis is another symptom of a declining America, the fall of an empire…

Nicholas Jay Boyes
Milwaukee Wisconsin
American Democratic Republic
12 8 2007

On American Economic Conditions 12 16 2007 by Nicholas Jay Boyes

"The U.S. central bank has lowered its benchmark interest rate three times since mid-September as a housing downturn, tightening credit conditions, and steep food and energy prices threaten to push the U.S. economy into recession.

"But cutting rates can have the unwanted side effect of pushing up prices, so the Fed finds itself in a tricky position of trying to revive growth without spurring inflation.

Reuters
Sun Dec 16, 2007
12:02pm EST

The lowering of interest rates means less surplus value for the bourgeoisie, as the interest rate is a direct marker of the amount of exploitation of the worker. It is unclear how much money the central bank loans to banks at low rates. If the number was high enough, it would be speculated on, like all debts of the state, i.e. national bonds, which are speculated on, often used by bourgeois governments to profit. By doing this they take the moneys of the state and use them to create surplus value...

Given the drive to keep the state indebted it is unlikely the central bank, under the control of the bourgeoisie, could possibly be a creator of wealth for the state, like recycling. More likely it is a cost, and paid for by tax dollars. When viewed in this light, any lowering of interest rates to banks would only shift money now in the hands of the state, being speculated on with the bond market, to more bourgeois control in the form of interest bearing capital. Any moves to lower the interest rates by the banks would lower their surplus value, as the mortgages are pegged to a given degree of exploitation of the proletariat, and also speculated on.

Inflation is another mechanism for increasing surplus value, as wages fall faster than the minimum wage rises. This can be detrimental to the economy if workers are too impoverished to survive on minimum wage, resulting in less labour being able to be accomplished. This too is speculated on in currency markets, with the value of the universal standard, wages paid at the minimum level, the minimum wage, being used as a reason to sink money in to a currency, to speculate on how much inflation can rise until the proletariat is too impoverished to work in a decent healthy condition....

Thus we see a connection in interest rates and inflation, as both are used to create more surplus value. Lowering of interest rates is a lowering of profit, inflation keeps down wages.

"Last week, U.S. data showed that wholesale inflation rose at the highest rate in 34 years, while consumer prices rose the most in more than two years.

"Greenspan repeated his assessment that the probability of a U.S. recession had moved up toward 50 percent but noted that corporate America's debt levels were in good shape, which should help cushion the blow from tightening credit terms.

Ibid. See above

Alan Greenspan led the central bank for 18 years, and is considered to be a good judge of bourgeois economic conditions in the United States.

The combination of rising inflation and higher consumer prices is a recipe for misery for the proletariat. Higher consumer prices, partly due to inflation means less commodities can be bought for the same amount of money. It creates surplus value for the bourgeoisie, but it would seem this time they misjudged the ability of the labourer to shoulder the burden of capital, and now they are being forced to change interest rates, lowering the exploitation rate of the labourer. Perhaps it was more politically popular than simply raising the minimum wage, which would also affect the housing market.

Of course, one could argue the homeowner is not on minimum wage, instead is a middle class or petty bourgeois shopowner. In this case it makes life for the labourer worse to give money to the homeowner. Of course, the average family in America has a mortgage or an inherited house, is a family, and is either workers with seniority or has skilled labourers in the commune. Thus to give money to the home mortgagee is the same as raising wages, only for the skilled labourer, and for the worker who is being paid more, i.e. union labour.

Alan Greenspan acknowledges the cutting of interest rates here is "a blow" to corporate America, in a rare statement. Usually the interest rate cuts are portrayed as helpful to the bourgeoisie, as they allow banks to loan more money. The only way they could help "corporate America" is too make them sell more loans faster, making up for the low prices. Of course, if inflation rises too much there are no longer consumers for the mortgages, resulting in less surplus value…

Nevertheless the tightening of the central banks is a lowering of the rate of exploitation of the labourer. Inflation can be caused by printing too much money, something the fed controls. The printing of money is directly related to inflation, as more currency on the market makes the money worth less, as currency is more dear it is worth more. This our bourgeois economist does not explain….

"Greenspan said real estate prices will stabilize only when the overhang of unsold new-construction homes begins to ease, and estimated that financial losses could be in the range of $200 billion to $400 billion as securities tied to failing subprime mortgages lose value.

Ibid.

A crisis in the financial bourgeoisie. Short term financial gain in sub prime mortgages, reliant upon the ability of the labourer to buy a home on low wages failed, and now to many homes are in the market with too few buyers. At the same time about a million men are pauperized to the brink of starvation, homeless due to the foul condition of American industrial conditions. Most of them will never be able to buy a home, especially not a new one like Greenspan is referring too. Thus we see an economic crisis, with the goods being offered, i.e. homes, but no one able to afford them, like a full stocked store and no customers…

Given the nature of the crisis, it looks like a protracted economic crisis is looming for America, with a recession almost inevitable. As I previously stated raising wages could ease the crisis, and that is what Greenspan is essentially proposing with his money given to homeowner to pay off mortgages. Unfortunately for the bourgeoisie it may be too late, if the houses are already foreclosed on too many workers, and there are not enough mortgages left to speculate on due to foreclosures…

Nicholas Jay Boyes
Milwaukee Wisconsin
American Democratic Republic
12 16 2007

On Iran and the United States by Nicholas Jay Boyes 12 6 2007

It certainly is strange to hear the turn the talk about Iran by the United States has taken recently. As little as 6 months ago the Americans were talking about defending Eastern Europe from rogue state Iranians building nuclear weapons. They even went so far as to suggest placing anti ballistic missile systems in the ex Soviet Union for this purpose, to stop Iran.

Now we get the latest reports from the National Intelligence Estimate (NIE) that suggests Iran is no longer trying to build a bomb, and if they ever were they abandoned it about 5 years ago.

It is troubling given the threats by George II to unleash World War Three if Iran gets the bomb. His own government now says that there is no threat from Iran, a complete turnaround.

With decisions like these it should be no surprise that even according to the bourgeois press his approval rating in the United States is 34%, with 59.5% disapproving of him.

The really pathetic part there is no real opposition in the country to replace George II. The only other party, the Democratic Party, is completely controlled by the same bourgeoisie. In most elections less than half of the Americans even bother to vote, and the average person is not as stupid as commonly thought.

The same leader was not even elected by the popular vote when he assumed control of the White House in 2000....

According to the same bourgeois press, FOX News, Congresses approval is even lower, with only 22.5% of Americans approving of congress, and a 67% disapproval rating.

Clearly the proletariat is not as easily taken as the men in charge would have us believe. The masses are not fooled by the empty promises of democracy from the leader of the Army and State, the Commander in Chief George II.

The last elections for congress seem to have placed the Democrats in power in congress, but they have disappointed the proletariat. With less than a quarter of people approving of the Congress it makes one wonder if anyone will even bother voting in the next election for president. Obviously the bourgeoisie is not giving up any power to the labourers, elections or not, even if the leader is a woman...

The gullible Russian people who gave up the dictatorship of the proletariat for free market free world economics must not read the American press. If they did they would see a quite a bit different picture of the New World than is commonly portrayed.

About the only bright part about this is that we see the American workers are clearly not fooled by George II, who speaks like a labourer, and lives on a ranch in Texas.

On the contrary they are put off by the macho Texan image, and see no improvement with the party of the opposition in Congress.

At least the proletariat in the United States knows he is being taken advantage of for production for capital...

If there was opposition in Russia to America by Vladimir Putin, you would think there would be some vocal opposition to the attempts to militarize the East of Europe by the American bourgeoisie. Of course, Putin is not that strong of a leader, and the only opposition is the Kommunist Party of the Russian Federation. The latter surely oppose the efforts to conquer the old Soviet Union with missile bases, but lack power due to the expropriation of the proletariat from production if Russia by the current government.

There are many in the United States who would simply like the NIE on Iran to go away, and choose to criticize it for being inaccurate. This is disappointing.

It is about time the people who are responsible for gathering information about foreign countries got it right. The Iranians do not need nuclear power, as they have petroleum. Nevertheless they can make fools of themselves by pursuing this course without threatening their neighbor as it is their right.

We should applaud the frankness of these reports, and the courage to stand up for what is the truth for a change by the NIE people. The proletariat will not be fooled by George II's violent attempts to conquer the Middle East with free markets.

Nicholas Jay Boyes
Milwaukee Wisconsin
American Democratic Republic
12 6 2007

On Venezuelan Columbian Relations by Nicholas Jay Boyes 12 28 2007

Hugo Chavez has begun to take a more active role in negotiations with the guerrilla Marxist movement in Columbia. Given the more than half a billion dollars sent every year by America to increase the potential for free trade and free markets, by military means, the latter what Americans call freedom would seem to be a stake in Columbia.

For about two generations, 40 years, the Columbian workers and peasants have been fighting for a Marxist revolution. Their national conditions are that of a guerrilla movement, a secret battle from the countryside with little or no support from any other powers in South America, with only their convictions of a belief in equality to guide them.

Hugo Chavez, regardless of the circumstances by which he came to power, not as a guerrilla but as a politically elected leader, now is starting to involve himself in the conflict, in prisoner exchanges. Hugo Chavez's move is a good step for the movement, and could significantly raise the hopes of a Marxist Columbia, by freeing prisoners on both sides of the conflict, and promoting a peaceful alternative to the decades of war.

The antithesis of Marxism is secrecy, which forces the proletariat into fear of open discussion of the bourgeois conditions he is forced to exist under.

The Columbian movement should come above ground a little, and openly discuss its goals for Columbia. Of course, it hinges on the moderating of Colombian President Alvaro Uribe, who is a bourgeois supporter of the regime of George Bush in America, and has fought against the peasant revolution. Thus we see Hugo Chavez coming into the scene, as his country is directly bordering Columbia to the East....

The role of Chavez should be to find a way the two sides can jointly govern Columbia, rather than the seemingly endless battle after battle that is becoming a stalemate in the Columbian South. Ecological

Socialism could be a force in Columbia, a movement of the peasants and proletariat, in the cities and countryside. It requires leadership, and Chavez could be in the right place at the right time to get both sides to compromise, and play a role as the international middle man between both sides.

Chavez has been trying to build a democratic socialism in Venezuela for about a decade now, and although at first it seemed like he wasn't serious now that he is getting involved in Columbia, the real thing, a Marxist revolution, it might be time for increased acceptance of him as a socialist leader by the Communist Party.

A dream of a peaceful Columbia is possible, although it may mean though that some regions of the country are allowed to have regional autonomy. The reliance on the cocaine trade has to stop, as it is damaging the ecology, and the coffee crop is reliant on clean water that is polluted making cocaine.

The growing of coffee remains the main export of Columbia, whose beans are par excellence.

The cocaine trade is often blamed on the revolution, and it is unclear if these accusations are correct or not, given the aggressive capitalist nature of the black market lumpen proletariat of America. The cocaine trade is an embarrassment to Columbia, and should be replaced by a more ecological and sustainable agriculture, even if it is export oriented like coffee.

Drugs and violence are the main things that are secrets to the proletariat, and the keeping of secrets in a revolution of mind and culture often creates conditions ripe for the bourgeoisie to suggest communism is a secret, which ultimately allows for them to easily rule with ignorance, even using the oppressed worker to oppress things in his own better interest, in particular labor unions and the socialist movement by the American Army soldier who comes from the working class.

It is a powder keg when they realize they are being used for a purpose that contradicts their own convictions, and the more lies that come from the bourgeoisie to maintain their control over the workers only inflames the conflict worse….

Hugo Chavez would be best to continue his efforts in Columbia. He will gain acceptance by the international proletariat by labouring in his own backyard, and then he will be able to speak from experience in a real revolution.

Nicholas Jay Boyes
Milwaukee Wisconsin
American Democratic Republic
12 28 2007

On the Objectives of War by Nicholas Jay Boyes 12 21 2007

The objectives of war are simple: first, declare war and enter the disputed territory. Next, after having occupied the country, take from it what you want, i.e. archeological artifacts. Next, having accomplished this, set the conquered people to work for the purpose of producing goods for the conquering country.

This has been the goal of warfare for a long time now, and historically the modern era has not changed even from the feudal conquering days i.e. the Crusades.

Thus one is given to wonder: when will George II set the Iraqi people about creating surplus value in Iraq for the American bourgeoisie?

It would seem that the oil must be of relevance, as this is the way the machinery is going to have to run on petroleum. Unfortunately the region where the oil is was turned into a war zone, and radioactive Depleted Uranium weapons used over a large area.

Thus we must ask the question of if the oil has the same value on the market with the radiation that it has to have picked up, under the radioactive ground in Iraq where the battles for the oil wells took place, or, if the oil is safe under the ground, what happens when the pipeline has to traverse a radioactive path to the sea for transport to America.

It would seem in any case it is going to be radioactive, and there really is not much known about what happens when man is exposed to small amounts of radiation frequently. All we know is no amount is not damaging to the health, and the oil and its value would have to be affected by this.

By this logic we see the difficulty of the position of the Americans, who now must set about creating industry in Iraq, and the only source of energy for industrial expansion a questionable source of fuel.

George II is going to have to present investment opportunities for the bourgeoisie in America, as they are clamoring for taxes to pay for the Iraqi adventure in Congress constantly. The same soldiers who fought in the war are going to be workers when they return, and the burrowed money from the war is going to have to be paid back by them, i.e. the bond market. Where is the surplus value George II has most likely promised the bourgeoisie? How is he going to set the Iraqi people about working in a climate of constant violence against the Americans?

All reasons for war aside, revenge, fear of attacks with missiles, etc., the fact of the matter is there is going to have to be a lot of work done to Iraq, and if the Americans cannot make a profit off it, it seems unlikely they will proceed in investing capital in it.

Much of the current debates in Congress must revolve around this, with the Democratic Party beginning to back down on continuing the war, undoubtedly many believing there is nothing but a bucket with a hole in the bottom in the Iraq spending....

As we have seen the oil becoming less valued due to radiation could occur, as it is not possible to clear the areas radiated in the war with Geiger counters. The desert has sandstorms, and the DU is buried under a meter of sand. It will never go away, and the longer it is there the more radioactive the oil in the ground is becoming. An unprofitable business adventure...

Nevertheless any efforts to clean up the damaged desert ecology must be welcomed, and the American should have to clean up or at least try, even though it will never go away, to remove the DU from the desert. How is something we do not have science to do yet...

Clearly the Iraq war is not going well. Unless George II finds a way to sell the devalued oil, and put the Iraqis to work creating surplus value for the American bourgeoisie, the adventure is going to continue to be opposed by the Democratic Party. And unfortunately for George it would seem the only source of energy in Iraq is the radiated oil, burning it causing radiation hell for anyone downwind. A tricky predicament...

Nicholas Jay Boyes
Milwaukee Wisconsin
American Democratic Republic
12 21 2007

Chapter 9

On the Current Economic Crisis in America by Nicholas Jay Boyes 9 15 2008

The current economic crisis in the financial capital sector of the economy is growing. Fannie May and Freddie Mac, two very large government mortgage providers, have been nationalized due to their immanent failure (more on this later). Today Lehman Brothers, another company involved in mortgages declared bankruptcy, and the government is letting it fail.

The question of just what caused the initial stages of the crisis must be noted:

1) aggressive speculation on the housing market increased demand where there was none, resulting in a speculative bubble which has been loosing stream for almost a year now.

2) The loaning of money at a variable rate, with the speculation on the ability and or inability for a proletarian family to pay resulting in a foreclosure, in turn a quick source of capital to the speculator, and a bankruptcy by the proletariat.

In both of these cases it is obviously not the lack of a work ethic in the labourer, rather an exploitative relationship with the bourgeois that has led to this dismal state of affairs for the bourgeois.

The most intelligent thing done as of yet was nationalization of Fannie May and Freddie Mac. These two companies alone are responsible for a half trillion dollars in mortgages. In combination with this the nationalization of Indy Mac in California, the states largest bank, has been nationalized. The latter was due to runs on the bank, and there was no choice for the bourgeoisie but to partially relinquish control of it to the state…

The nationalization of these large banks is good for the labourer as it weakens the power of the financial bourgeoisie, whose fascist crotchets continue to be a detriment to the labourer.

The stock market is now sliding backward, and all American factories who are reliant on financial capital for their transactions are going to have to essentially ask the government for credit. It is still unclear what the government will do when they cannot pay. Expect more nationalization and shuttered industry…

As far as the individual homeowner, a change in mortgage payments is in order. A maximum of 30% of income should be the price of the mortgage, and the bank could stop asking for interest on the risky loans. To do otherwise is to further take advantage of the labourer who finally has been able to afford a home and to stop the foreclosures.

Thus far the federal government has not been too apt to prosecute the people who made off with money from the failed banks. It would seem in the interests of the labourer that the men who made fortunes off the variable rate loans be punished or at least return the money.

Of course, as in any great swindle, somebody always gets away with the gold, or no one would even try…

Nicholas Jay Boyes
Milwaukee Wisconsin
American Democratic Republic
9 15 2008

On the Economic Crisis in the USA by Nicholas Jay Boyes 9 18 2008

It is strange to hear the trouble in the financial markets, in the realm of financial capital, insurance, banks, etc in America. It would seem overnight the country is in a crisis comparable to the Great Depression. From the same free trade free market bourgeois who previously would not even call the brewing trouble a recession we now see panic, with the words depression becoming commonplace.

And not only America. Russia's newly founded stock market has fallen sharply, as well as Western Europe and Japan. It would seem many markets are all having trouble, and it is even effecting steel production.

"Steelmaker, Hit by Weak Demand, Plans to Cut $4 Billion in Costs Over Five Years...

"ArcelorMittal, the world's largest steelmaker by output, is ready to cut production by 15% or more in response to weaker demand.

"The Luxembourg-based steelmaker also unveiled a plan to cut $4 billion in costs in the next five years, through productivity improvements and by curbing energy consumption, which also suggests the company expects growth to slow.

ArcelorMittal To Reduce Output
September 18, 2008
The Wall Street Journal

It would seem the failure of the bureaucracies, i.e. insurance, banking, is having a far reaching effect. Arcelor Mittal cutting 15 % must be a major blow to the company, whose hopes are increasingly pinned on the control of output in the market, and relying on cutting production like the oil cartel OPEC in hopes of driving the price of steel up.

The obvious answer to the economic crisis in the long term is to increase recycling steel. A nationwide recycling programme would provide solid work for the proletariat hardest hit by the failure of the free market.

The aggressive free market ideas have left the economic system in shambles, and the companies are all failing due to the aggressive speculation in Wall Street, who drove the prices of commodities up in a bubble that has finally burst asunder. The companies obviously do not trouble themselves with who will now pay, they declare bankruptcy and either the state bails them out or the workers all lose their jobs.

It leads to the conclusion of why the state should pay back its debts. Why should not the state itself declare bankruptcy like the companies? The national debt is such a large number, $ 9, 649, 388, 025, 001. 54 as of writing 9 18 2008.

This translates too :

"The estimated population of the United States is 304,753,702 so each citizen's share of this debt is $31,662.91.

"The National Debt has continued to increase an average of $1.80 billion per day since September 28, 2007!

See US National Debt clock online.

Much of this is due to George II's war, which will ultimately be paid back by the soldiers who fought in it. They will be the workers who pay the 32 grand in their taxes to free Iraq of the weapons of mass destruction (not yet found after 5 years) that Tony Blair famously said would be striking London in 45 minutes...

At some point the state is going to have to declare bankruptcy. The average worker makes about half the amount owed by him in a year, and with the debt increasing 1.8 billion daily, increasing exponentially due to interest on the bonds, bankruptcy is inevitable.

When the fateful day comes the bourgeois will cry bloody murder. The worker will sigh a sigh of relief, and his burden will be lifted. The dead weight of the bond market will no longer tax the worker, revolution will have occurred...

Nicholas Jay Boyes
Milwaukee Wisconsin
American Democratic Republic
9 18 2008

On the Economic Crisis pt.3 9 22 2008 by Nicholas Jay Boyes

The economic crisis is widening again, with the highest rise in oil prices yet, 16$ a barrel today.

This comes on the heels of a massive government plan yet to be passed to sink 700 billion dollars into buying the failed loans of the banks who lent recklessly.

The plan calls for nationalizing the bad debt, and the people footing the bill for the transaction.

The proletariat always is made to pay when nationalization occurs it seems, even though it was their blood and sweat that created the commodity to begin with, and the capital that runs the machinery. In this case it is financial capital, the product of labour, commodities sold on the market and kept as capital by the bourgeois.

In the end nationalization is a good move as it weakens the power of the financial bourgeois who created the problem. Unfortunately the bail out literally is just this, paying bail to the system for the regardless of the fact the labourers were the victims. The bail for the end of the oppressive labour practices, a form of usury practiced by the bourgeois, the sub prime mortgage market, comes from the backs of the workers to the owners of the companies, a financial reward for the total failure of these keepers of capital to keep the economy functioning.

The next question is just what exactly the state is going to do about the interest on these bad loans. Interest on the debts if they are owned by the state is another form of taxes, as it is the labourers paying the state again for what they should own themselves.

The issuing of bonds is another form of surplus value, as it speculates on the debts of the state, a favorite tactic of reactionary bourgeois governments. It makes the young people ultimately shoulder the burden of the prosperity of the owners of capital enjoy as credit. The worker who turns old enough to labour is immediately saddled with a mountain of debt when he begins labouring. If bonds are to be issued for the bad debt, the companies might as well have just been allowed to fail, and capitalists fall flat on their gorgeous faces...

The state making interest on the mortgages makes society the capitalist. Why would the labourer whose money is paying for the bailout ask himself for interest? Obviously he is only paying more. Again, why would the proletariat require any surplus value on his mortgage? Any money made is the collective product of labour, and thus we see the fallacy of even selling the mortgages at a surplus.

Real nationalization, ending the interest payments on the mortgaged capital, not issuing any bonds or expecting to ever sell the capital nationalized is the only favorable route for labourers. Otherwise is only to further reward this class of swindlers on Wall Street and their speculations on the labour of men.

The rise in the price of oil is another aspect of the financial crisis. The oil companies to make money could simply buy a ton of oil, store it a year, break it out, and make massive profits.

Needless to say this has been thought of, and even discussed by congress. Yet total inaction on the part of these citizens of power, short of unnationalizing the oil in Iraq, from the state under Saddam Hussein to the oil companies like Exxon Mobil, is what we see.

Not that the state under Mr. Hussein let much of the money go to the people anyways, judging by the palaces he inhabited. Nevertheless the Iraqi people had a better shot at controlling the resource under their feet when it was nominally Iraqi National oil...

The actions of the bourgeois in the next few days will be crucial. Nationalizing the companies failing is a good step, but the price tag is just giving away money to the men who caused the problem to begin with. And the bond market is rewarding capitalists for the good deeds of the labourers who could be in control of the money through a workers state at some point. The highest government salary is the president: $400,000. Are the culprits of the cause of the problem going to be allowed to walk with the states money in the form of salary greater than the leader of the state? Fiscal and moral bankruptcy...

Nicholas Jay Boyes
Milwaukee Wisconsin
American Democratic Republic
9 22 2008

On the Economic Crisis in America 11 6 2008 by Nicholas Jay Boyes

What started as it seemed was a small problem in the market, excessive speculation on the ability of people, primarily workers, to pay for mortgages has spread to the entire market, and even the world market.

In the past two days the Dow Jones Industrial Average has fallen almost 10%. One would think the election in America, one of the most heavily voted in and watched for years in the making, and the new leader who followed, would give the market confidence. Instead it appears the election of Barak Obama, the first African American president, has shaken faith in the market.

It was not the first day of trouble for the economy though. The market has been falling for almost a year now, and is worth about half it was last year. It seems every day it either rises a few percent or continues falling dramatically.

There are many reasons for the economic decline, from speculation on adjustable rate mortgages (the interest rate rises after purchase), to the inability of the largest economy in the world, the United States, to make a metric conversion.

The latter may be trivialized by some, not a real indicator of economic well being, but approached scientifically it should be obvious the less advanced machinery produced in America is going to be rejected by metric countries.

The logistics of getting parts shipped from across the sea every time a part breaks is the barrier to industrial development in America today.

It doesn't look like the bourgeois are all that ready to fix it, either. The new president elect never even mentioned this, a metric conversion for America. It is not clear how the most pressing problems of the average proletariat can be missed, even by a more average type of guy like Barak Obama. John McCain also never even mentioned the need for a conversion…

Today it was the car companies lining up to get money out of the state, 25 billion dollars worth of loans. Apparently their profits were not high enough on the dinosaurs of the Sports Utility Vehicles, leading to the failure of their industry the minute gas was rising in value.

Gas is about the only thing worth less, primarily due to the president lowering the standard for pollution from the vehicles. One wonders how much the health of the people who inhabit the cities near the highway, or have to travel on it, is worth. Is it being speculated on by the private health care system? Perhaps a rising premium for an aspiring young bourgeois?

So first the financial capitalists start to decline, with the banking industry hardest hit as too many people are in the adjustable rate mortgages, and unable to pay. The speculation on their ability to be saddled increasingly with debt, and then the inability to sell the properties after they have been foreclosed on leads to the failure of the financial bourgeoisie. Did they expect to buy the houses and again resell them?

This results in a 700 billion dollar bailout for the banking industry by Congress, to the same people who sold the adjustable rate loans with the hopes of making a profit off denying a proletariat his ability to own a home by foreclosure and sale of the home for surplus value.

There is one road we are not seeing as regards the bourgeoisie. It is sink or swim. The proletariat is not helped by huge bailouts of the financial bourgeoisie, or state giveaways to the non metric dinosaurs of the integrated steel mills and the auto industry.

The free traders always told the labourer if the company was unprofitable the jobs would be axed. Now they come to the people in Congress asking for massive loans and other mechanisms for extracting large amounts of capital.

Sink or Swim. There is no reason why the labourers should be expected to keep afloat the companies affected by the bad economy when it was their fault they got themselves and everyone else in to the crisis.

Nicholas Jay Boyes
Milwaukee Wisconsin
American Democratic Republic
11 6 2008

On the Economic Crisis 11 17 2008 by Nicholas Jay Boyes

Clearly the economic crisis is spiraling out of control. The companies are forced to cut higher paying jobs, especially union jobs. They do this to make capital, something in short supply these days. The effect of this on the community is that it is harder for the workers who have been removed from their jobs where seniority and the union meant they could afford their mortgages.

Once the labourers who could no longer afford their mortgages on a lower non union wage, at a non union factory, their houses began being foreclosed on by the financial capitalists.

Had it been a small number of foreclosures, the economic system could have swept it under the rug. This was not possible as the bourgeois all started doing it (cutting union jobs), and next thing we knew there was crisis. Too many foreclosed homes, and the inability of the homes even to be sold because everyone was working low paying jobs and the crisis was formed.

The bourgeoisie originally planned to sell adjustable rate mortgages so they could profit off foreclosure, but eventually no one could afford the houses even with a fixed rate as no one had any money. Their union jobs had all been removed, sent to Mexico, etc.

The crisis then began to spiral out of control, with the financial capitalists who owned the mortgages first hit. This led to the necessity of nationalization of the mortgage industry.

Fannie Mae and Freddie Mac, the companies who owned the mortgages, were made the property of the state. This was a logical move. It was this or failure of the system altogether, and massive foreclosures. The state was the alternative, with its deep pockets a guaranty of the ability to take losses.

Of course, it was capitalists who caused the problem by removal of the unions, and the high paying jobs through free trade. It was an act of kindness to nationalize the financial capital in this case. It was this or face the wrath of millions of oppressed labourers with nothing to do or in service jobs.

The deeper the crisis the more union jobs lost. Every capitalist used the crisis as an excuse to remove better paid labourers, and remove seniority. This eventually led to other sectors of the economies failure, first the automobile industry. They went hat in hand to the government as noone could afford to buy their vehicles on a lower wage. This ceased to make the company a competitive industry, and we have yet to see but expect higher tariffs as the monopoly condition of the subsidized industry forms. It is not free trade, it is dumping, something socialist economies are often faulted with...

As the crisis deepens the goods on the shelves are ceasing to be bought. Goods collecting dust do not create demand, as they are not sold. Production begins failing, and the goods are still on the shelves. An eerie sort of shadow economy of a bourgeoisie who can still pay for the goods, and luxuries. Obviously everyone is not going to be able to work producing luxury items for a small group of those who own capital...

Thus we see the spiraling effects of the economic crisis, spreading to the world market, entirely the fault of the oppressive tactics of the free traders. The world market, the prime achievement of capitalism, is melting down....

Nicholas Jay Boyes
Milwaukee Wisconsin
American Democratic Republic
11 17 2008

On the Economic Crisis 11 25 2008 by Nicholas Jay Boyes

The economic crisis is forcing the bourgeoisie to use taxpayers money to bail out countless large banks, and is even attracting the car industry to ask for the capital the government has. The money comes as taxation on the individuals no one thinks of in these trying times, the proletariat at his industrial job. The moneys are spent to make up for the foolishness of the financial bourgeoisie, whose questionable lending practices have totally failed.

Just what the bailouts are going to achieve is still not known. The failed loans were the responsibility of the financial bourgeoisie and it is their lending processes that have left the companies totally bankrupt, only to be rescued with tax money.

A logical course of action would be to stop supporting these ships of fools who created the financial problem to begin with. Cutting them loose and focusing on the industries that are coming forward for the government money would seem to be the best hope to help the proletariat.

If the auto makers need to have 25 billion dollars, why should they not simply be given 25 billion dollars worth of orders for passenger trains, buses, etc. These expenditures are already made by the state, as these are not capitalist companies. There is no reason why GM, Chrysler and Ford could not be making buses with the 25 billion dollar bailout.

The unfortunate we truth about the bourgeoisie is they are basically giving blank checks too the financial capitalists. The banker receives a billion dollar check from the treasury and is told to spend wisely.

Naturally the stock market rises, free money always generates an orgy of capital....

Simply giving the companies most affected by the crisis orders to build state industrial machinery, something they should be capable of doing, is the logical conclusion if the state money is going to be used as capital.

Constantly giving the state money to the financial companies is taxation without representation. The proletariat is not helped by these massive expenditures to prop up the bourgeoisie whose attempts to make capital have caused the crisis to begin with. A falling stock market to the worker looks like less surplus value in production, the goal of all revolution. Ending the bonds of surplus value is emancipation of the proletariat. Labour is in bondage to the financial bourgeoisie, and they are now using the state money to maintain their control over the labour process.

At some point the tipping point is going to be reached when it becomes impossible to bail out the companies any longer. They will have to sink or swim. Given the free traders who once moved jobs overseas to make more capital, this should not be foreign. They were the most brutal in the loss of union jobs to the less developed world, where wages are a pittance.

Real state orders for real state machinery, not for war but to recycle, build passenger railroad, etc. is the only reason the money should be used for bailing out anybody. The bailout asks the oppressed proletariat to shoulder the burden of the financial bourgeoisie whose failures have resulted in this mess.

Nicholas Jay Boyes
Milwaukee Wisconsin
American Democratic Republic
11 25 2008

On the Economic Crisis 12 16 2008 by Nicholas Jay Boyes

"The Fed has already reduced the overnight federal funds rate by 4.25 percentage points, to 1 percent, since September 2007.

"It also has engaged in a degree of quantitative easing by pumping more than $1 trillion into financial markets, inflating the money supply and almost doubling the size of its balance sheet over the past year.

"The rapid increase in the supply of money in normal times might stoke fears of inflation. But that seems a distant problem at a time when banks are reluctant to lend.

"In fact, some economists predict the United States could suffer a deflationary period in 2009, as tumbling oil and commodity prices, alongside increasing slack in the economy, deliver a sustained fall in general prices.

Reuters
12 16 2008

To begin with, the inflation rate rises when the quantity of money increases from the Central Bank. The money becomes devalued as the additional money printed is worth less.

The reason generally that the bourgeois do this is to lower the cost of labour. When the value of money decreases, wages fall.

Nominally wages remain unchanged, but the value of the money falling in real terms makes the wages fall.

This is why it is ridiculous for Reuters to suggest there will not be inflation due to the increased printing of money by the bourgeoisie. Inflation is inevitable, and the use value of a commodity exchanged even for less money remains the same.

Exchange value can be affected by printing more money, but it is not the commodity affected except for the less wages paid for it. The means of exchange, the dollar, is simply worth less.

Commodity value is only affected by the reduced cost of labour required to pay for it.

Thus the Central Bank under the bourgeoisie is again sticking it to the labourers to pay for their failures. Lowering of the lending rate is also connected, as the rate of lending goes below the inflation rate, resulting in easy profits for capitalists. The Central Bank is literally paying capitalists to lend in this case...

The value of commodities only drops due to the amount of labour required to produce them under normal conditions. The means of exchange may be variable, but this only nominally changes the value of the commodity. Commodity value is the value of the labour and the constant capital, machinery, raw materials, etc. required to produce the commodity.

If the value of wages fall due to inflation it is unclear how our political economist expects the wage labourer to be able to purchase commodities, resulting in a general lowering of demand. In this case perhaps the prices would fall, but result in crisis as the goods stacked up in port, i.e. autos in Los Angeles currently.

The point is if the value of wages falls, caused by the Central Bank printing more money, inflation, how can this ease the crisis? Less wages means less purchases. Less purchases, lower demand. Factories begin to experience over production. The goods are on the shelves but nobody is buying.

The Central Bank is not helping the proletariat by causing inflation. Even if they do lower the cost of commodities it is unclear how in a climate of lowering demand the economy would even be helped. Less purchasing power means less ability to buy commodities by the labourer. Less purchases is the same thing they are trying to fix, As purchases raise the value of commodities, and cause a reduction in over production.

Nicholas Jay Boyes
Milwaukee Wisconsin
American Democratic Republic
12 16 2008

On the Economic Crisis by Nicholas Jay Boyes 1 27 2009

In the near past, the last century in particular, there was a criticism of nationalized industry that went like this:

State industry is a monopoly, as it is reliant on state money and thus sets prices.

This argument, taken further, also alleges the currency is devalued as the cost of labour is no longer commensurate to the commodity produced.

It would seem to be a valid argument. Given a condition of competition, with little or no state intervention in the economy, it almost seems logical. Of course, in reality something different is occurring.

To begin with, the object of monopoly is to drive out all competition, and be the largest supplier of a commodity. Thus it is not to remove profit, the goal of nationalization.

This having been said I move now to the idea of giving state money to private industry, as both presidents Bush and Obama have and are currently doing.

The effect of this is encouraging monopoly, as these companies are no longer directly competing. The smokescreen of a company being solely viewed as a source of jobs also comes into play. A company is judged by its ability to make a profit. This is the real reason for investment by shareholders.

If a company were judged by how many workers it had instead of how much surplus value it produces it would be an incentive to lower profit by simply hiring more labourers to do the same job, for political power....

It is becoming increasingly more difficult in a failing capitalist system totally reliant on state taxation and bonds to justify private property. The fear of the state subsidizing and driving out competitors through nationalization, would seem to be very close to what Obama is doing with private industry. The companies are no longer solely reliant on competition to set prices, and the money of the people is increasingly being used to prop up failing capitalist projects. How does one compete with the endless pockets of the state? The system of private property and competition seems to be completely reliant on the money taken by taxation without representation on the companies ownership directors to give the bourgeois the ability to make surplus value at the expense of the labourer.

And just which private industries are to get the money? The potential for corruption would seem rather high. It must be almost irresistible to give friends money, and the opposition none. Good thing everybody thinks Obama is an honest man...

Nicholas Jay Boyes
Milwaukee Wisconsin
American Democratic Republic
1 27 2009